Nalopakhyanam
The Science of Victory

Translated from Sanskrit by
Christine Devin

—

General Editor: Kireet Joshi

Discovery Publisher

Author: Christine Devin
General Editor: Kireet Joshi

616 Corporate Way
Valley Cottage, New York
www.discoverypublisher.com
editors@discoverypublisher.com
Proudly not on Facebook or Twitter

New York • Paris • Dublin • Tokyo • Hong Kong

Acknowledgement

This book is part of a series of monographs centered on three values: Illumination, Heroism and Harmony. The research, preparation and publication of those books are the result of the work and cooperation of several research teams of the Sri Aurobindo International Institute of Educational Research (SAIIER) at Auroville.

General Editor: Kireet Joshi

Author and compiler of this monograph: Christine Devin

We would like to thank all those who helped in the publication of this book. The task of producing learning-teaching material for integral education in its highest and broadest sense, was very close to Kireet Joshi's heart. It was his wish that these books be made available to a large number of students and teachers.

NALOPAKHYANAM
THE SCIENCE OF VICTORY

TRANSLATED FROM SANSKRIT BY
CHRISTINE DEVIN

—

GENERAL EDITOR: KIREET JOSHI

ILLUMINATION, HEROISM AND HARMONY

Preface

The task of preparing teaching-learning material for value-oriented education is enormous.

There is, first, the idea that value-oriented education should be exploratory rather than prescriptive, and that the teaching-learning material should provide to the learners a growing experience of exploration.

Secondly, it is rightly contended that the proper inspiration to turn to value-orientation is provided by biographies, autobiographical accounts, personal anecdotes, epistles, short poems, stories of humour, stories of human interest, brief passages filled with pregnant meanings, reflective short essays written in well-chiselled language, plays, powerful accounts of historical events, statements of personal experiences of values in actual situations of life, and similar other statements of scientific, philosophical, artistic and literary expression.

Thirdly, we may take into account the contemporary fact that the entire world is moving rapidly towards the synthesis of the East and the West, and in that context, it seems obvious that our teaching-learning material should foster the gradual familiarisation of students with global themes of universal significance as also those that underline the importance of diversity in unity. This implies that the material should bring the students nearer to their cultural heritage, but also to the highest that is available in the cultural experiences of the world at large.

Fourthly, an attempt should be made to select from Indian and world history such examples that could illustrate the theme of the upward progress of humankind. The selected research material could be multi-sided, and it should be presented in such a way that teachers can make use of it in the manner and in the context that they need in specific situations that might obtain or that can be created in respect of the students.

The research team at the Sri Aurobindo International Institute of Educational Research (SAIIER) has attempted the creation of the relevant teaching-learning material, and they have decided to present the same in the form of monographs. The total number of these monographs will be around eighty to eighty-five.

It appears that there are three major powers that uplift life to higher and higher normative levels, and the value of these powers, if well illustrated, could be effectively conveyed to the learners for their upliftment. These powers are those of illumination, heroism and harmony.

It may be useful to explore the meanings of these terms – illumination, heroism and harmony – since the aim of these monographs is to provide material for a study of what is sought to be conveyed through these three terms. We offer here exploratory statements in regard to these three terms.

Illumination is that ignition of inner light in which meaning and value of substance and life-movement are seized, understood, comprehended, held, and possessed, stimulating and inspiring guided action and application and creativity culminating in joy, delight, even ecstasy. The width, depth and height of the light and vision determine the degrees of illumination, and when they reach the splendour and glory of synthesis and harmony, illumination ripens into wisdom. Wisdom, too, has varying degrees that can uncover powers of knowledge and action, which reveal unsuspected secrets and unimagined skills of art and craft of creativity and effectiveness.

Heroism is, essentially, inspired force and self-giving and sacrifice in the operations of will that is applied to the quest, realisation and triumph of meaning and value against the resistance of limitations and obstacles by means of courage, battle and adventure. There are degrees and heights of heroism determined by the intensity, persistence and vastness of sacrifice. Heroism attains

the highest states of greatness and refinement when it is guided by the highest wisdom and inspired by the sense of service to the ends of justice and harmony, as well as when tasks are executed with consummate skill.

Harmony is a progressive state and action of synthesis and equilibrium generated by the creative force of joy and beauty and delight that combines and unites knowledge and peace and stability with will and action and growth and development. Without harmony, there is no perfection, even though there could be maximisation of one or more elements of our nature. When illumination and heroism join and engender relations of mutuality and unity, each is perfected by the other and creativity is endless.

The present monograph is entitled *The Science of Victory*. This ancient story by the poet-Rishi Vyasa recounts how heroism guided by wisdom enable two human beings, crushed by adverse circumstances, to emerge victorious from a terrible ordeal. Since they are intensely pure and sincere, they can, even at the worst moments, remain open to luminous intuitions; they can keep their strength and courage; they let themselves be guided at all times by an invisible hand. By constantly invoking a higher force, they place themselves under its protection and they keep their mind and heart open to its action — a force which is actively present in the universe and which pushes towards justice, harmony and unity. This is an extraordinary demonstration of how, by clinging to the golden thread of love and faith, one can traverse the whirlpools and dangerous undercurrents of the river of life and reach the other shore, on the firm ground of joy and freedom.

* * *

THE SCIENCE OF VICTORY

Introduction

इतिहासमिमं श्रुत्वा पुराणां शश्वदुत्तमम्
पुत्रान् पौत्रान् पशूंश्चापि लभते नृषु चाग्र्रताम् ।
आरोग्यप्रीतिमांश्चैव भविष्यति न संशयः ।।

"Whoever listens to that ancient and excellent story will get everything that his heart desires, there is no doubt about it." (Mahabharata, Vanaparva, 79-16)[1]

A Lesson on Life

The story of Nala and Damayanti (Nalopakhyanam), as told in the Mahabharata, seems to begin and end like a fairy tale. Yet what happens in between is anything but a fairy tale — if we give this word the meaning of something remote from real life. On the contrary, this is a universal story containing some of the deepest truths about life.

---

1. Literally: "will get sons, grandsons, cattle, honour, health and happiness".

This is about two exceptional human beings, placed in ideal circumstances: the king Nala and the princess Damayanti. It starts with a very pure love between them which is put to the test by the gods themselves. Their marriage is followed by a life of harmony and happiness. Then suddenly the smooth path is interrupted. A crack appears in this beautiful picture and widens more and more. An evil being named Kali enters the king, clouds his judgement and leads him to all kinds of disasters, including loss of his kingdom, exile, separation from the children, parting from his wife, loneliness, suffering and servitude for both of them.

Evil, doubts, pain, separation have appeared in the story of Nala and Damayanti, indeed as they often appear in our own life. For how many lives on this earth are not chequered lives? One rises, one falls; one gains, one loses. Rama is all set to be crowned King of Ayodhya and at that very moment he is sent into exile. Shakuntala awaits her marriage and then she is cursed by a Rishi and forgotten by her lover. Vishvamitra is about to reap the fruit of thousands of years of tapasya when he gets angry and loses everything in a second. Rare are the linear lives in which upheaval of some kind does not take place.

What does one need for going undefeated through all this? What makes some people sink and other people emerge stronger? And if it is true that the life of a man is a "search after pure Truth and unmixed Bliss", what are the helps in *this search? And if it is true that human life is susceptible to deviation, how can those deviating forces be conquered?*

How can we learn the art of Victory?

Since it contains many secrets about this art. or rather this science, the story of Nala and Damayanti is considered an invaluable lesson in human life.

Like all those to be found in the ancient epics of India, this tale contains great knowledge. The poets who wrote them did not intend merely to tell a tale in a beautiful or noble manner or to create an interesting poem, although they did this with great success. The Mahabharata and the Ramayana are itihāsa, that is to say, they are "an ancient historical or legendary tradition turned to creative use as a significant mythus or tale expressive of some spiritual or religious or ethical or ideal meaning and thus formative of the mind of the people." (Sri Aurobindo) Valmiki and Vyasa indeed shaped the minds of the Indian people. They were architects and sculptors of life. Their epics contain a deep reflection on life, on human psychology, on society, politics and religion. If the Mahabharata has been spoken of as a fifth Veda, it is because it is not only a great poem, it is also a body of knowledge.

धर्मे चार्थे च कामे च मोक्षे च भारतर्षभ ।
यदिहास्ति तदन्यत्र यन्नेहास्ति न तत् क्वचित् ।।

> *"Whatever is in this book, pertaining to the four human interests: dharma, personal gain, passion or liberation, is elsewhere [in the world]; whatever is not in the book does not exist anywhere [in the world]."[1]*

The work of these epics was to popularize the discoveries of the great minds and souls of India through stories:

> *"That which was for the cultured classes contained in Veda and Upanishad, shut into profound philosophical aphorism and treatise or inculcated in Dharmashastra and Arthashastra, was put here into creative and living figures, associated with familiar story and legend, fused into a vivid representation of life and thus made a near and living power that all could readily assimilate through the poetic word appealing at once to the soul and the imagination and the intelligence."[2]*

The Vedic Rishis spoke of life as a battle between the forces of light and the forces of darkness. They said that some forces help you in this battle, and that other forces obstruct you.

1. Adiparva, 2.20.
2. Sri Aurobindo

They said that life is a sacrifice, and that as you burn your imperfections in the fire of sacrifice, you can move upwards, you progress from untruth to truth. They spoke of Rita, the right law of action originating in the vast consciousness of truth; and from that concept had come the idea of dharma. Those Vedic notions are present in the Mahabharata, brought out from an inner plane to an outer plane (ideas, ethics, politics), although in the tale of Nala and Damayanti (which is probably a very old story), they still keep their ancient and inner significance.

Indeed this is how the story is presented to us in the Mahabharata: as an ancient tale containing secrets which can help men overwhelmed with doubt and sorrow; as an example pregnant with meaning; as a demonstration of the significance of life. From the story of Nala and Damayanti, it is said in the Mahabharata, Yudhishthira, like all men plunged in a great crisis, could draw benefit.

"Was there ever a man more miserable than me?"

"Never was there a more miserable man than me", kept repeating Yudhishthira. He was a king, and he had lost his kingdom. He was the elder and the wisest brother; he was regarded as Dharma-raja, a model of moral rectitude, and now he was being accused of bringing misfortune upon himself and his family by not resisting the lure of gambling.

Even his closest friends reproached him for pledging himself, his brothers, and even their wife, on the gambling board. Time and again that fateful scene would come back to his mind when, through his own fault, the proud Draupadi was dragged by her hair into the assembly hall and publicly humiliated, like no other woman had ever been. How could he sleep when he relived that moment, remembered his helplessness and the sarcasm of his enemies? He had been trapped by an expert in the art of cheating and made to play dice while he himself did not know the secret of this game (अनक्षज्ञस्य हि सतो 52.44). And what was in store for him now? He had gambled and lost; now, as per the agreement he had to live a life of exile in the forest along with his brothers and their wife. As if this was not enough, his dearest brother, the great Arjuna himself had left for a far-off region in the north in quest of the science of divine weapons. When would he return? Would he ever return?

Yudhishthira felt so lonely. How much he missed the presence of the compassionate Arjuna! How unbearable to hear over and over the harsh words of his brother Bhima! And what should he answer when, impatient with what he saw as passivity, Bhima pressed him to break his word and take arms against their enemies? "You will gamble again anyway, this is certain. Even after all that has happened, you will not be able to refuse the game!" taunted Bhima. It hurt so much! Sorrow and shame seared Yudhishthira's heart and dried his mouth. At night, unable to find rest, he kept tossing on his bed of torture and bitterly lamented over his misery. "No, indeed, never was there a more unfortunate man than me."

One day a great sage, one of those Rishis who lived in the forest-hermitages of ancient India, appeared where the brothers lived. They all welcomed him according to tradition. After some time, Yudhishthira found him alone. He sat at his feet and bared his heart to him. His pain, his worries, his doubts, his helplessness, he all confided to the great Rishi. And he concluded with the one thing that seemed to him a certainty in his ocean of miseries, "Was there ever a king more miserable than me?"

"Yes, there was", answered the Rishi gently. "Once upon a time there was a king who was more unfortunate than you. He was alone in the forest, separated from his wife, without brothers or friends, much more lonely than you are. He was not even able to reflect on dharma as you do, because his mind was clouded. If you want to listen to that ancient story, I will tell you about the king Nala who had to bear a greater ordeal than you and who triumphed over his miseries."

This is how the story of Nala and Damayanti is introduced to us by the great poet Vyasa in the Vanaparva of the Mahabharata: as a tale of courage and endurance in the face of adversity; as an example of what fate can do to man and what man can do to fate; a lesson of hope given to a man who is very close to falling prey to despair. Through this story, the

Rishi wants Yudhishthira to have a deeper understanding of the play of invisible forces in life. He reminds him that there are times in one's life when one can become a plaything in the hands of some of those forces, which are out to obstruct and destroy; but he shows him how, even in these circumstances, one can be protected and guided by some other forces, and how one can get free from one's fear and destructive sense of guilt by surpassing one's limitations and ignorance. For the central idea in the poem is that of the spirit of degeneracy, the genius of the iron age: an evil being suddenly takes hold of a man who till that day had been an ideal of purity and loyalty, brings all kinds of calamities into his life, but eventually is overpowered by a steadfast conjugal love. Nothing more tonic and refreshing for the soul than this tale of two capable minds struggling with hardships and difficulties. Nothing more strengthening than the story of this two-headed hero whose aspiring and unconquerable spirit ultimately triumphs. Nothing more elevating that the story of this unwavering love, pure and strong enough to make a man and a woman pass through some of the worst crises one can ever meet in life, and emerge victorious.

"In the same way as Nala regained his kingdom, you also will meet good fortune again," promised the Rishi to Yudhishthira after telling the story.

"Considering that men's gains are always unstable, one should not be perturbed by success or failure."

अस्थिरत्वं च संचिन्त्य पुरुषार्थस्य नित्यदा ।
तस्योदये व्यये चापि न चिन्तयितुमर्हसि ।। **79.12**

"The apprehension you have that you will be again invited by an expert in the game to play dice, that fear I will destroy."

भयात् त्रस्यसि यच्च त्वमाह्वयिष्यति मां पुनः ।
अक्षज्ञ इति तत् तेऽहं नाशयिष्यामि पार्थिव ।।**79.18**

The lesson will not be lost on Yudhishthira: he will express his desire to learn from the Rishi Brihadashva the science of dice and also the science of horses, thereby taking the initiative in the battle of life and getting rid of his fear.

* * *

Damayanti

Damayanti, "the one who subdues, or conquers", is the name of Nala's wife. And she does conquer; by the purity and sincerity of her love, the tremendous strength of her will-power, her deep insight into the complexities of life and knowledge of the right action, obstacles are removed; seemingly insurmountable difficulties are surmounted; evil forces are defeated. There is a special quality to all her actions, a certain golden touch as it were. At each turn of the story Damayanti solves the inextricable, straightens what is bent, snatches victory from the jaws of defeat.

Her love for Nala is no ordinary love, it is a love of the soul as symbolised in the image of the swan, the golden-winged messenger through which the two lovers communicate. The truth of this love is so deep that it even won over the gods.

What made Damayanti choose Nala over the gods? Four heavenly beings, Indra, Agni, Yama and Varuna had asked for Damayanti's hand. They had even used Nala as their emissary, and Nala, although a suitor himself, had faithfully helped them. Yet Damayanti chose Nala, a man, over the gods. Why? What does Nala have that the gods do not have? Here, a clue to the question is hidden in the beautiful image of the four gods seated along with Nala at the swayamvar[1] ceremony.

---

1. A ceremony during which the young girl garlands the man whom she chooses for her future husband.

The gods have all taken the appearance of Nala so that the five beings seated side by side look exactly alike. Which one is the real Nala? How is Damayanti going to recognize him and select him as her husband? Damayanti directly addresses the gods — तेन सत्येन विबुधास्तमेव प्रदिशन्तु मे *— and the truth of her love is so compelling that it forces them, as it were, to help her in identifying Nala: suddenly she is able to perceive the differences between the five figures in front of her. The gods are not soiled by dust or sweat. Their garlands are unfading, their eyes unwinking. Their feet do not touch the ground. They cast no shadow. In contrast Nala's feet stand on the ground; he has a shadow; his garland is fading; one can see sweat on his forehead and dust on his body, and his eyes blink. What does this symbolic and poetic language signify? Gods are stable, immobile, always luminous, invariably harmonious. Time does not change them, struggle does not affect them. In a word, these gods belong to a static, non-evolutionary world. Nala's world, on the contrary, is the world of the earth, which his feet touch; it is an evolutionary world, not all glorious and harmonious, consisting of light and shadows, of sweat and dust, of struggle and impurity. A world where everything moves and changes, the way his garland fades with the passing of time. Yet in that imperfection, there is an urge towards a higher and more many-sided perfection. This urge, this need is the sign of the soul. Gods are not thirsty. The human soul is. It searches for truth, freedom, unmixed bliss. That thirst is* *what leads the soul in its voyage towards greater and greater lights. This is the experience Damayanti seeks: the travel of the soul towards greater and greater perfection. It is why she chooses Nala. Not for her a static and contented perfection. Her robust soul seeks the adventure and the struggle and an all-embracing triumph.*

That aspiration towards perfection is what guides Damayanti and leads her ultimately to victory. When, finding herself alone in the jungle, she cursed Kali, the evil being that robbed Nala of his senses, the purity of her love turned her curse into an effective weapon, potent enough to strike at Kali and deliver Nala from its influence. Kali himself later confirmed this,

इन्द्रसेनस्य जननी कुपिता माशपत् पुरा ।
यदा त्वया परित्यक्ता ततोऽहं भृशपीडितः । ।**72 .34**

> *"Indrasena's mother, Damayanti, cursed me in anger when she was abandoned by you. Therefore I have been suffering greatly."*

It can be observed that there is not the slightest taint of egoism in this love: Damayanti never ever feels sorry for herself, never indulges in self-pity: even alone in a wild and dangerous forest, even in the grasp of a huge python, she thinks only of Nala's suffering, she grieves only for Nala, she has compassion only for Nala.

Again, this psychic love is what finally would indicate to Damayanti, more surely than any external sign, that she was going to be reunited with Nala. Back in her father's home, one day she felt a sudden and tremendous joy; that was the language of the soul, making her understand more clearly than from any spoken word that, at last, she was going to meet her beloved. The cry of the peacock (unfortunately omitted in Sister Nivedita's version), symbol of Victory, confirmed to her that her ordeals were over.

According to the ancient Indian science of yoga and its knowledge of the subtle body, the centre of the will is located between the eyebrows. It is interesting to note that Damayanti is said to have a birth sign between the two eyebrows. Could this physical sign be a symbol of Damayanti's indomitable will? One is inclined to believe so, for Damayanti's will-power is indeed unshakable: neither the gods' offer prior to the swayamvar, nor Nala's departure, nor her grief or her fear made her deviate for one second from her path, which is the path of total self-giving to Nala. Once she gave herself to Nala, — and that was even before she ever saw him, — she was ready to die rather than live without him. And after she was separated from Nala, she lived with only one aim, to find him again. When after her adventures she finally returns to her parents' house, the author does not describe her relief at being again reunited with her family and children, he does not linger on domestic scenes of happiness. There is no rest or respite for Damayanti. She is still the same woman Nala abandoned in the forest: she is clothed with only one garment; her hair is untied; she is covered with dust; and she thinks only of one thing: how to find Nala, how to let him know that she is waiting for him, how to make him come back to her. She respects her elders like any educated woman of the time and, before acting, she asks her parents for their permission, but her will is so strong, her intention is so clear that her parents cannot but let her act the way she has decided to. In this way, she is a totally free woman, and one can sense the empathy of Vyasa's "granite mind" with the formidable strength of this character.

More than her purity and her will-power maybe, what makes Damayanti an exceptional human being, is her deep understanding of human life coupled with her knowledge of the right action. She was a young girl whose universe till her marriage must have been confined within the walls of the palace, and yet she felt and acted as if she had lives and lives of experience behind her. Right from the beginning of the tragedy she had understood that Nala was not himself, that some dark force had taken hold of him and that he was a victim; it is why she never ever blamed Nala. She could perceive that his judgment was clouded, that he was *mohita* and unable to decide clearly and freely. Similarly, when they wandered in the forest, on her insistence Nala promised that he would not *abandon her, but she knew that although he meant what he said, he would not be able to keep his word since he was not master of his mind anymore.*

अवैमि चाहं नृपते न तु मां त्यक्तुमर्हसि ।
चेतसा त्वपकृष्टेन मां त्यजेथा महीपते
। ।61.33

*"I understand, O king, you could not leave
me. But because of your mind which is pulled
in another direction, you could very well
abandon me."*

She did not put a name onto the hostile force, she did not know that it was an evil being called Kali, but she was aware of its presence and of its effect on her husband.

Not only does she know the power of love and truth, as we have mentioned already when we noted that she forced the gods to accept her choice, not only does she know the power of dark forces such as the one which took possession of her husband, not only is she conscious of the battle between those contradictory pulls, but she is also desha-kaal-jnaa: (60.12) she knows how to act decisively at the right moment and at the right place. While Nala gambled and one by one lost all his possessions, she, foreseeing what was going to happen, acted swiftly and saved her children. Later, back in her father's capital, after more than three years of ordeal, she devised ways to find Nala and, once he was found, to make him come. The detailed instructions she gave to her envoys and each word of the message she wanted them to spread, the idea of the second swayamvar and the announcement made at such a short notice, the four tests she made Nala undergo in order to be able to declare irrefutably that this ugly charioteer indeed was Nala — all her plans and the way she carried them out reveal the extraordinary gift of Damayanti: emotions never come in the way of action; she has a clear vision of what has to be done and she executes the action calmly, thoroughly, with an utmost care and with a great attention to details.

Such is the character portrayed so powerfully and yet with such remarkable simplicity by Vyasa.

It would be tempting to declare that she is the main protagonist of the story, and that her role is even more important than that of Nala. But this would be unfair to the man Damayanti chose of her own will amongst gods. In fact, Nala and Damayanti were attacked by the same enemy, waged the same battle, although through different means, and they both won.

Nala

Nala's truthfulness was equal to that of Damayanti. Lest we be inclined to think of Nala as a husband who betrays his wife, right at the beginning of the story we are shown how firm he is in his clinging to the truth: he promised the gods he would help them and he did it, whatever the consequences for himself. He was entirely transparent, and spoke nothing but the truth, be it in front of the gods or in front of Damayanti. In fact, he was so pure and sincere that Kali, after resolving to take possession of him, had to wait for twelve full years as he could not find any opening, any flaw that would allow him to sneak in. After twelve years, a minuscule fault was committed that gave Kali the opportunities he sought. From then onwards, Nala was not himself.

However, even with his mind confused and torn, the one thing that remained always present, albeit in the background, and acted as a protection was his love and respect for Damayanti. Like Yudhishthira, he was invited to stake his wife on the gambling board. Nala's only answer, recounts Vyasa, was to silently remove all his ornaments and walk out of the palace. Even in the forest, when he agonised over the action to be taken, even at that moment when his mind was dola iva, *pulled like a swing in two opposite directions, he never questioned the purity and fidelity of Damayanti and knew that those would be her protection.*

In the concluding chapter of the story, Nala fully conscious of what happened to him, pointed out to Damayanti,

मम राज्यं प्रणष्टं यन्नाहं तत् कृतवान् स्वयम् ।
कलिना तत् कृतं भीरु यच्च त्वामहमत्यजम् ।।76.17
"That my kingdom was lost and that I abandoned you was all the work of Kali, it was not my doing."

Kali, adds Nala, was burnt by Damayanti's curse "like fire burnt by fire", and "was defeated by my endeavours and tapasya" — मम च व्यवसायेन तपसा चैव निर्जितः 73.20 — ।
What were Nala's efforts to defeat Kali and overcome the deep crisis in which he had been plunged? It would be too long to list all of them but we would like to underline three stages in his tapasya that were crucial in his battle against darkness and which were all the more heroic since they were undertaken in the backdrop of extreme sorrow, overwhelming feeling of guilt and physical distress.

The first is the easiest to detect: the act of compassion towards another being. In the jungle, Nala succours the Karkotaka snake caught in a ring of fire. Due to a curse this cobra could not move. He is encircled by flames, cries for help and finally is saved by Nala who carries him to a safer place. Then a strange thing happens: in return for this kindness, Karkotaka bites Nala. This apparent act of ingratitude is in reality a great boon, as the serpent himself explains it to

Nala. Firstly, the poison that has entered Nala will torment Kali so much that ultimately he will have to come out of him. Secondly, this bite has the immediate effect of transforming Nala's appearance. His beauty has disappeared. His face has become black. And this is for Nala's own good, as is clear from Karkotaka's utterance:

ततः कर्कोटको नागः सान्त्वयन् नलमब्रवीत् ।
मया तेऽन्तर्हितं रूपं न त्वां विद्युर्जना इति ।।66.14

"*Then reassuring Nala, the cobra Karkotaka told him: 'I have made your form disappear so that no one can recognize you.'*"

So it is clear from the text itself that Nala did not become ugly because of Kali's entering him. The change in Nala occurred much after this event. It was effected by the snake with the specific purpose of helping him. In fact, this transformation is the beginning of the process of recovery. From that moment, "no one could recognize you", said the snake. This leads us to the second stage in Nala's tapasya.

The second step in his tapasya is his period of Ajñātavās. On the advice of Karkotaka, Nala goes to Ayodhya. There, under the name of Bahuka, he proposes his services to the king Rituparna. He will look after the horses of the King. So here is Nala, unrecognizable, with a different face, in a foreign land, among strangers. It seems to us that these periods of retreat

*[Ajnātavās] described in the Indian epics, when one hides in
an unknown place under an assumed identity, symbolically
indicate an inner movement of introspection, a time devoted
to a deep inner quest and renewal. All energies are necessary, a
great concentration is necessary, a dialogue with the innermost
part of one's being is necessary. Space and time are required,
solitude is a help. The last thing one needs is interference from
others, howsoever good-intentioned they may be. Karkotaka
has made sure that "no one can recognize" Nala; his living in a
distant land makes it impossible for him to be confronted with
past acquaintances. He is alone, facing his own life, engaged
in a dialogue with his soul. And each evening he sings his love
for his beloved: a single verse, a beautiful and simple shloka,
repeated again and again, as a mantra, a cry from his heart:*

क्व नु क्षुत्पिपासार्ता श्रान्ता शेते तपस्विनी ।
स्मरन्ती तस्य मन्दस्य कं वा साद्योपतिष्ठति ।।**67 .10**

   *"Where resteth she that roamed the wood
   Hungry and parched and worn, but always true?
   Doth she remember yet her faultful lord?
   Ah, who is near her now?"*

*The last decisive step for Nala is the decision to learn the
science of counting from the King Rituparna. Both the King
and Nala are on their way to the capital of Vidarbha. They
have heard that a second swayamvar ceremony for Damayanti*

will take place shortly. While driving, Nala asks Rituparna to teach him the science of counting. As soon as he learnt it, Kali came out of him — तस्याक्षहृदयज्ञस्य शरीरान्निसृतः कलिः **72.30** —. This is also a symbol and one presumes that the science of counting indicates the quality of discrimination acquired by Nala. After all, samkhya (number) is the name of a branch of Indian yoga. The choice of the tree whose leaves and fruits Nala is taught how to count, is significant since it is the Vibhitaka tree, "the tree which removes fear", also called "the dice tree", its fruits being used in the game of dice.[1] By learning discrimination, by widening his consciousness Nala had gotten rid of his fear. The significance of "dice" has been turned upside down.

The Nalopakhyanam has the charm of a beautiful fairy tale and the fierce and stern power of an epic. While portraying the characteristics of Vyasa's poetry, Sri Aurobindo dwelt at length on the characteristics of two works which are not part of the original Mahabharata and are yet by the same hand: Nala and Savitri. Says he: "Here we have the very morning of Vyasa's genius, when he was young and ardent, perhaps still under the immediate influence of Valmiki (one of the most

---

1. *Terminalia belerica.* Sanskrit names: Bibheetaka or Vibheetaka (regular use eliminates fear of disease), Aksha (the seeds are used in a game of gambling, Kalivriksha (the tree of Kali), Bhootavas (animals take shelter in its shade). See *Ayurvedic Pharmacology and Therapeutic Uses of Medicinal Plants* by Vaidya V.M. Gogte, Bharatiya Vidya Bhavan, Mumbai, 2000, p. 438-39.

pathetic touches in the Nala is borrowed straight out of the Ramayana), at any rate able, without ceasing to be finely restrained, to give some rein to his fancy. The Nala therefore has the delicate and unusual romantic grace of a young and severe classic who has permitted himself to go a-maying in the fields of romance. There is a remote charm of restraint in the midst of abandon, of vigilance in the play of fancy which is passing sweet and strange. ... This then is the rare charm of these two poems that we find there the soul of the pale and marble Rishi, the philosopher, the great statesman, the strong and stern poet of war and empire, when it was yet in its radiant morning, far from the turmoil of courts and cities and the roar of the battle-field and had not yet scaled the mountain-tops of thought."[1]

While this story contains the wonders and the touches of the miraculous that pertain to a fairy tale, it has for subject, like all Indian epics, a struggle between two ideal forces, universal and opposing. One can read the story as a parable which, by means of very ancient symbols, tells us the adventure and battles of man's inner being led from darkness to light by the sheer power of love. What Nala and Damayanti experienced at the very start of the story, the deep emotion that caught hold of them, as wonderful and fresh and miraculous as the blooming of a flower, as undeniable and compelling as the

---

1. Sri Aurobindo, Notes on the Mahabharata, Vol III, Centenary Edition, Pondicherry, 1972, pp. 153-4.

sunrise, was the promise of their attaining an even greater joy, widened, deepened and illumined by the fire of their aspiration.

THE SCIENCE OF VICTORY

The story of Nala and Damayanti
as retold by Sister Nivedita

Once upon a time there was a king named Nala, who ruled over a people known as the Nishadas. Now this Nala was the first of kings. In person he was strong and handsome, full of kingly honour, and gracious in his bearing. He loved archery and hunting, and all the sports of monarchs. And one special gift was his, in an extraordinary degree, the knowledge, namely, of the management of horses. Thus in beauty, in character, in fortune, and in power, there was scarcely in the whole world another king like Nala.

If there were one, it could only be Bhima, King of the Vidarbhas, a sovereign of heroic nature and great courage, deeply loved by all his subjects. Now Bhima had three sons and one daughter, the Princess Damayanti. And the fame of Damayanti, for her mingling of beauty and sweetness, and royal grace and dignity, had gone throughout the world. Never had one so lovely been seen before. She was said to shine, even in the midst of the beauty of her handmaidens, like the bright lightning amidst the dark clouds. And the hearts of the very gods were filled with gladness whenever they looked upon this exquisite maiden.

It happened that constantly before Damayanti, the minstrels and heralds chanted the praises of Nala, and before Nala those of Damayanti, till the two began to dream of each other, with an attachment that was not born of sight. And Nala, conscious of the love that was awakening within him, began to pass much of his time in the gardens of his palace, alone. And it came to pass that one day he saw there a flock of wild swans with golden wings, and from amongst them he caught with his hands one. And the bird was much afraid, and said, "O King, slay me not! Release me, and I will go to Damayanti and so speak to her of thee, that she will desire to wed thee, and no other in the world!" Musing, and stroking the wings of the swan, Nala heard his words, and saying, "Ah, then do thou indeed even so!" opened his hands, and let him go free.

Then the swans flew up and away to the city of the Vidarbhas, and alighted in the palace gardens before Damayanti and her maidens. And all the beautiful girls scattered immediately, to run after the fleeing birds, trying each to catch one. But that after which Damayanti ran, led her away to a lonely place, and addressed her in human speech. "Peerless amongst men, O Damayanti!" it said, "is Nala, King of the Nishadas. Accept thou him! Wed thou with him! Ever happy and blessed is the union of the best with the best!" The Princess stood with head bowed and folded hands, as soon as she understood what the swan would say; but when he ended, she looked up with a smile and a sigh. "Dear bird!" she said, "speak thou even thus unto him also!"

And the hand-maidens of Damayanti, from this time on, began to notice that she grew abstracted. She wandered much alone. She sighed and became pale, and in the midst of merriment, her thoughts would be far away. Then, delicately and indirectly, they represented the matter to Bhima, and he, reflecting that his daughter was now grown up, realised that her marriage ought to be arranged, and sent out messages all over the country, that on a certain day her Swayamvara would be held.

From every part, at this news, came the kings, attended by their body-guards, and travelling in the utmost splendour, with horses and elephants and chariots. And all were received in due state by Bhima, and assigned royal quarters, pending the day of Damayanti's Swayamvara. And even amongst the gods did the news go forth, and Indra, and Agni, and Varuna, and Yama himself, the King of Death, set out from high heaven for the city of the Vidarbhas, each eager to win the hand of the Princess.

But as the proud gods went, they overtook a mortal wending his way on foot, and his beauty and greatness, of mind as well as body, were such that they immediately determined to leave their chariots in the skies, and tread the earth in the company of this man. Then, suddenly alighting before him — for the gods know all — they said, "Nala! thou art a man to be trusted. Wilt thou promise to carry a message for us?"

Nala, seeing four luminous beings appear before him, and hearing them ask him to be their messenger, answered immediately, "Yea! That will I!" and then, drawing nearer, he added, "But tell me first, who are ye who address me, and what is the message, further, that I should carry for you?" Said Indra, "We are the Immortals, come hither for the sake of Damayanti. Indra am I. Here at my side is Agni, God of Fire. There is Varuna, Lord of Waters. And next to him stands Yama, destroyer of the bodies of men. Do thou, on our behalf, appear before Damayanti, saying, 'The Guardians of the World are coming to thy Swayamvara. Choose thou, I pray thee, one of the gods for thy lord!' "

"But," said Nala, "I myself am come hither with the selfsame object. How can a man plead with the woman whom he loves on behalf of others? Spare me, ye Gods!

Send me not upon this errand!".

"Then why, O King!" answered the .gods gravely, "didst thou first promise? Why, having promised, dost thou now seek to break thy word?"

Hearing this, Nala spoke again, saying, "But even if I went, how could I hope to enter the apartments of Damayanti? Is not the palace of Bhima well guarded?"

But Indra replied, "Leave that to us! If thou wilt go, thou shalt have the power to enter!" And saying "Then, O Gods, I obey your will!" Nala found himself, on the moment, in the presence of Damayanti, within the private apartment of the palace of Bhima.

Damayanti sat amongst her ladies. The next day was to be her Swayamvara, and feeling sure that Nala would attend it, the smiles had come back to her lips, and the colour to her cheeks. Her eyes were full of light, and the words she spoke were both witty and tender. Seeing his beloved thus for the first time, Nala felt how deep and overflowing was his love for her. Truly, her beauty was so great, that the very moon was put to shame by it. He had not thought, he had not heard, he could not even have imagined, anything so perfect. But his word was given, and given to the gods, and he controlled his own feeling.

This determination did not take even so much as that instant which it required for him to become visible to the assembled maidens. As he did so, they sprang to their feet in amazement, feeling no fear, but struck with wonder at the beauty of the spirit who appeared thus before them, and full of the question, "Who can it be?" Yet were they too shy to venture to speak to him. Only Damayanti came forward gently, and smilingly addressed the heroic vision,

Encounter between Nala and the gods

saying, "Who art thou? And how hast thou contrived to enter unperceived? Are not my apartments well guarded, and the King's orders severe?"

Hearing these words, the King answered, " My name, O Princess, is Nala. I have entered here undiscovered, by the power of the gods. I come as their messenger. Indra, Agni, Varuna, and Yama, all alike desire, O beauteous one! at the morrow's Swayamvara to be chosen by thee. As their messenger, I say, 'Choose thou one of them for thy lord!'"

Damayanti bowed as she heard the names of the gods. Then, with a smile, she turned herself to Nala. "Nay, O Hero!" she answered, "it is not the gods, but thee thyself whom I shall choose. Thy message reached me, borne hither by the swans. Thee have I accepted in my heart.

The "invisible" Nala entering Damayanti's apartments

For thee has the Swayamvara been called. Failing thee, I refuse to be won by any!"

"Nay," answered Nala, "in the presence of the gods, wouldst thou choose a man? Ah, for thine own sake, turn thy heart, I pray thee, to those high-souled lords, the creators of the worlds, unto the dust of whose feet I am not equal! Misguided is the mortal who setteth them at nought. Be warned, I beg of thee. Choose thou one of these heavenly beings. What woman would not be proud to be sought by the protectors of men? Truly, do I speak unto thee, as thy friend!"

Tears were by this time running down the cheeks of Damayanti. Trembling, and standing before Nala with folded hands, she answered, "I bow to the gods, but thee, O King, have I chosen for my lord!"

"Blessed one!" answered Nala gently. "Do even as thou wilt. How dare I, having given my word to another, turn the occasion to my own profit? Yet, if that had consisted with honour, I would have sought my will! Knowing this, do thou decide."

The face of Damayanti had changed as Nala spoke these words. Under the tears were now smiles. For his secret was told. A moment she stood and thought, and then she raised her head. "I see a way, O Monarch," she said, "by which no blame whatever can attach itself to thee. Come thou to the Swayamvara with the gods. Then, in their presence, shall I choose thee. And the choice will be mine alone. Thou shalt be without sin."

Nala realised nothing, save the promise that Damayanti on the morrow would give herself to him. With throbbing pulses, but quiet manner, he bowed his head in farewell, and, immediately becoming once more invisible, returned to the presence of the gods, and told them all that had happened. "The maiden said to me, 'Let the gods, O Hero, come with thee to my Swayamvara. I shall, in their presence, choose thee. Yet shalt thou be without sin.' " And the gods accepted the report of their messenger, for he had been faithful to his trust.

* * *

**The Gods on their aerial chariots,
on their way to Damayanti's Swayamvara**

The morning of the Swayamvara dawned brightly, and the kings entered the lofty portals of the amphitheatre, even as lions might enter into the mountain wilds. The scene was all magnificence. Amongst the great pillars sat each royal guest on a shining throne. Each bore his sceptre and turban of state. Each was surrounded by his own heralds and minstrels, and amongst the blaze of silks and banners and jewels shone the flowers and foliage that decorated the hall.

At the appointed hour, preceded by her trumpeters, and surrounded by her escort, the Princess Damayanti entered. And her loveliness was such that, to the

**The Swayamvara:
Damayanti arriving in front of the five Nalas**

assembled monarchs, she seemed to be surrounded with
dazzling light. All drew in their breath, and remained
almost without stirring, at the sight of such matchless
beauty. One by one the names and achievements of each
monarch were proclaimed. The heralds of the Princess
would challenge, and those of each king in turn would
reply, and Damayanti stood listening, ready to give the
signal, when her choice should be made.

But when the name of Nala was called, and she raised
her head and looked up, before stepping to his side, what
was not the terror of Damayanti to find that there, seated
side by side on different thrones, all equally splendid, all

equally noble, were no less than five Nalas, and she had no means of distinguishing him whom she would choose?

The Princess looked and tried to choose. Then she hesitated, and stepped back. Then she tried again, but all to no purpose. She knew of course that this was a trick of the gods. Four of these five were Indra, Agni, Varuna, and Yama. One was Nala. But which one? She tried to remember the marks of the celestial beings, as they had been told to her in her childhood by old people. But none of these marks did she see on the persons before her, so exactly had they all reproduced the form of Nala. What must she do? At this supreme moment of her life she dared not make a mistake.

Pondering deeply in her own mind, it suddenly occurred to Damayanti that she should appeal for protection to the gods themselves! Immediately, bowing down unto them in mind and speech, and folding her hands reverently, she tremblingly addressed them:

"From that moment, O ye Gods, when I gave ear to the words of the wild swan, did I choose Nala, the King of the Nishadas, to be my lord. That I may be true to this, let the gods now reveal him to me! Inasmuch as neither in thought nor word have I ever yet wavered in that resolve, oh, that I may hereafter be true to it, let the gods now reveal him to me! And since, verily, it was the gods themselves who destined the King of the Nishadas to be my lord, let them now, that themselves may be true to themselves, reveal him to me! To Nala alone did I vow to give myself. That I may be true to this vow, let them now reveal him to me! I take refuge in the mercy of the exalted Guardians of the Worlds! Let them now resume their proper forms, that I may know my rightful lord!"

Touched by these pitiful words of Damayanti, and awed by her fixed resolve and her pure and womanly love, the gods immediately did what they could, in that public place, to grant her prayer, by taking back, without change of form, their divine marks. And straightaway she saw that they were not soiled by dust or sweat. Their garlands were unfading, their eyes unwinking. They cast no shadows. Nor did their feet touch the earth. And Nala stood revealed by his shadow and his fading garlands; the stains of dust and sweat; his standing on the ground, and his human eyes. And no sooner did Damayanti thus perceive the difference between him and the gods than she stepped forward eagerly to fulfil her troth.[1] Stooping shyly, she caught in her left hand the hem of Nala's garment, and then raising herself proudly, she threw round his neck a wreath of beautiful flowers. And all present, seeing her thus choose the one human Nala for her husband, broke out into sudden exclamations, and the gods themselves cried, "Well done! Well done!"

---

1. troth = pledge.

And Nala stepped down from his high place, and said, "Since thou, O blessed one, hast chosen me, a mortal, front the midst of the Immortals, know me for a spouse to whom shall thy every wish be sacred. Truly do I promise thee, that as long as life lasts I shall remain thine and thine alone!" And so with mutual vows and homage, they both sought and received the protection of the gods. Then did all guests, royal and divine, depart; and the marriage of Nala and Damayanti was performed; and they went, in great happiness, to the city of the Nishadas.

Now as the gods were returning to their own regions, they met Kali, the King of Darkness, and Dwapara, Spirit of Twilight, coming to the earth. And when they asked where they were going, Kali replied, "To Damayanti's Swayamvara. My heart is fixed on wedding with that damsel." Hearing this, Indra smiled and answered, "But her Swayamvara is already ended. In our sight she hath chosen Nala for her husband." To this said Kali, that vilest of the celestials, in great wrath, "If, spurning the Immortals, Damayanti in their presence hath wedded with a mortal, then is it meet she should suffer a heavy doom!" But the gods answered; "Nay, with our sanction was it that Damayanti chose Nala. And what damsel is there who would not have done the same? Great and manly and learned, that tiger amongst men, that mortal who resembles one of the Divine Protectors, has truthfulness and forbearance and knowledge, and purity and self-control, and perfect tranquillity of soul. Whoever, O Kali, wisheth to curse this Nala, will end in cursing and destroying himself by his own act!"

Having spoken thus solemnly, the gods turned, leaving Kali and Dwapara, and went to heaven. But when they had gone, Kali whispered to Dwapara, "I must be revenged! I must be revenged! I shall possess Nala, and deprive him of wife and kingdom. And thou, entering into the dice, shalt help me to do this!"

Yet was it twelve long years ere[1] Kali, watching Nala, could find in his conduct any slightest flaw by which he might be able to enter in and possess him. At last, however, there came an evening when he performed his worship without having completed all his ablutions. Then, through this error, Kali took possession of Nala. Also he appeared before his brother, Pushkara, tempting him to challenge Nala to a game of dice. And Dwapara also, at the same time, placed himself in the hands of Pushkara as the principal die. Such was the beginning of that terrible gambling that lasted month after month, and ended by depriving Nala of all that he had.

Many times, in the course of that play, came Damayanti and the citizens and subjects of Nala, and begged him to desist. But he, maddened by the indwelling Kali, turned

---

1. ere = before

a deaf ear to his Queen, and grew only the more intent upon the dice. Till she, seeing that evil was about to come upon them, sent for the royal charioteer. "O charioteer," she said, "I seek thy protection. My mind misgiveth me. The King may come to grief. Take thou therefore these my children, my son Indrasena and my daughter Indrasenâ, and carry them to my father's house. And when thou hast given them into the care of my kindred, do thou even as thou wilt." And when the royal councillors had been consulted, they found the bidding of the Queen to be good, and the children were sent to the care of Bhima.

And when the charioteer had gone, Pushkara won from Nala his kingdom and all else that was left to him. And laughing he said, "O King, what stake hast thou now? Damayanti alone remaineth. Let us play for her!" And Nala gazed at Pushkara in anguish, but spake never a word.

Then, taking off all his ornaments, and covered only with a single garment, leaving behind him all his wealth, the King set out to leave the city. But Damayanti, clothing herself also in one long scarf, followed after him through the gates. And for three days and nights they wandered together, without food and without rest. For Pushkara had made proclamation that any who gave help to Nala should be condemned to death; so that, partly for fear of the sentence, and partly lest they should bring further harm on their King himself, none of his subjects dared to offer them anything.

At last, on the fourth day, wandering in the forest seeking for roots and fruits, Nala saw some birds of golden colour, and thinking, "Here is food!" snatched off his one piece of clothing, and threw it over them to catch them. But lo! the birds rose upwards to the sky, bearing the garment with them! And then, looking down and beholding the once mighty lord of the Nishadas standing naked in the forest, his mind full of gloom, and his gaze rooted to the earth, the birds spake mockingly, and said to him, "Oh thou of little wit, we are none other than the dice with which thou playedst. We followed thee to take away thy garment. For it pleased us not that thou shouldst take with thee even a single cloth!" Hearing these words, and realising his terrible plight, since he had, it was evident, mysterious beings for his foes, Nala turned himself to Damayanti, and said over and over again, "Yonder, my gentle one, is the road to thy father's kingdom. I have lost all, Damayanti. I am doomed and deprived of my senses. But I am thy lord. Listen to me. Yonder is the road to thy father's kingdom."

But Damayanti answered him with sobs. "O King, how could I go," she asked him, "leaving thee in the wild woods alone, deprived of all things, and worn with hunger and toil? Nay, nay, whenever, in these ill-starred days, thy heart may turn to the thought of thy former happiness, thou shalt find me near thee, to soothe thy weariness! Remember what the physicians say, 'In sorrow is there no physic equal to the wife!' Is it not true, O Nala, that which I say unto thee?"

"O my gentle Damayanti," answered Nala, "it is even as thou sayest. Truly there is no friend, no medicine, equal unto the wife. But I am not seeking to renounce thee. Why dost thou tremble so? I could forsake myself, beloved, but thee I could not forsake. Wherefore, my timid one, shouldst thou dread this?"

But on Damayanti lay the prevision of the wife, and she answered, "I know, O King, that thou wouldst not willingly desert me. Yet maddened and distracted, many things are possible. Why dost thou repeatedly point out to me the way to my father's home? Or if thou really desirest to place me with my kindred, then let us wend together to the country of the Vidarbhas. Thou shalt there be received with honour by the King, and, respected by all, shalt dwell happily in our home." "Surely," answered Nala, "thy father's kingdom is to me even as my own. Yet could I not by any means go there at such a crisis. Once did I appear there in fortune, bringing glory upon thee. How could I go in this misery, causing thee shame?"

Talking together in this fashion, Damayanti had contrived to share her own clothing with her husband, and thus wandering slowly on together, they came to a shed reserved for travellers. Here they sat down on the bare earth to rest, and then, worn out with hunger and weariness and sorrow, both, unawares, fell fast asleep.

But Nala, whose mind was distraught by Kali, could not rest. As soon as Damayanti slept, he woke, and began to turn over in his mind all the disaster he had brought upon her. Reflecting on her devotion, he began to think that if only he were not with her, she would surely find her way to her father's kingdom. And out of the very honour in which he held her, it was unimaginable to him that she should be in danger on the way. Thinking thus, the question occurred to him, how could he cut their common garment without her being awakened by his act? And with this question in his mind; under the influence of Kali, he strode up and down the shed. At that very moment, he caught sight of a sword lying a step or two away, unsheathed. Seizing this, he cut the veil in half, and then, throwing the sword away, he turned and left Damayanti, in her sleep, alone.

Yet again and again, his heart failing him, did the King of the Nishadas return to the hut to look once more, and yet once more, at his sleeping wife. "Dragged away," says the chronicler, "by Kali, but drawn back by love," it seemed as if the mind of the wretched King were rent in twain,[1] and one half fought against the other. "Alas! alas!" he

_____
1. twain = two

lamented, "there sleepeth my beloved on the bare earth, like one forlorn! What will she do when she awaketh? How will she wander alone through the perils of these woods? May the Sun himself — thou blessed One! — and the Guardian Spirits, and the Stars and the Winds, be thy protectors, thy womanly honour being its own best guard!" And addressing thus his dear wife, peerless in beauty, Nala strove to go, being reft of his reason by Kali. Till at last, stupefied and bereft[1] of his senses, Nala forsook his sleeping wife. In sorrow departed he, maddened and distraught, leaving her alone in that solitary forest.

---

1. bereft = deprived

The adventures of Damayanti

We insert here a few original extracts from the Mahabharata. Damayanti finds herself alone in the jungle. The reader will find side by side the original Sanskrit and a translation.[1]

chap 63

बृहदश्व उवाच
अपक्रान्ते नले राजन् दमयन्ती गतक्लमा ।
अबुध्यत वरारोहा संत्रस्ता विजने वने ।।1।।
अपश्यमाना भर्तारं शोकदुःखसमन्विता ।
प्राक्रोशदुच्चैः संत्रस्ता महाराजेति नैषधम् ।।2।।

Brihadashva said

O King Yudhishthira! Nala had gone. Refreshed, the slender-waisted Damayanti wakened, shuddering at the wood's silence. When she did not see her husband, afraid and anguished she cried aloud and called the King: "Maharaj!

हा नाथ हा महाराज हा स्वामिन्किं जहासि माम् ।
हा हतासि विनष्टासि भीतासि विजने वने ।।3।।

---

1. It has been said that one could learn Sanskrit by reading this text again and again, as it is considered relatively simple to understand.

"Ha, lord! Ha, Maharaj! Ha, my prince! Why hast thou abandoned me? Ha, I am slain, I am doomed, I am frigtened in this lonely forest.

ननु नाम महाराज धर्मज्ञः सत्यवागसि ।
कथमुक्त्वा तथा सत्यं सुप्तामुत्सृज्य कानने ।।४।।

"Surely, O king thou wert true and just. How having spoken the truth couldst thou have abandoned me while I was sleeping in the forest?

कथमुत्सृज्य गन्तासि दक्षां भार्यामनुव्रताम् ।
विशेषतोऽनपकृते परेणापकृते सति ।।५।।

"I am thy diligent and faithful wife. I have not done any wrong to thee. If any wrong was committed, it was by others, not by me. So how couldst thou leave me ?

शक्यसे ता गिरः सम्यक् कर्तुं मयि नरेश्वर ।
यास्तेषां लोकपालानां संनिधौ कथिताः पुरा ।।६।।

"O king, the words that thou hast proclaimed in the presence of the gods [at the swayamvar ceremony], wilt thou be able to make them true to me?

नाकाले विहितो मृत्युर्मर्त्यानां पुरुषर्षभ ।
तत्र कान्ता त्वयोत्सृष्टा मुहूर्तमपि जीवति ।।7।।

"Death does not come to men except at the appointed time. This is the only reason why thy wife, although abandoned by thee, is still living for a moment.

पर्याप्तः परिहासोऽयमेतावान्पुरुषर्षभ ।
भीताहमतिदुर्धर्ष दर्शयात्मानमीश्वर ।।8।।

"Enough with this jest! This is enough, o best of men! I am afraid, o unconquerable. Show thyself, my lord.

दृश्यसे दृश्यसे राजन्नेष दृष्टोऽसि नैषध ।
आवार्य गुल्मैरात्मानं किं मां न प्रतिभाषसे ।।9।।

"I saw thee, I saw thee! King, I saw thee there, Naishadha. Having hidden thyself with creepers, why dost thou not answer me?

नृशंस बत राजेन्द्र यन्मामेवङ्गतामिह ।
विलपन्तीं समागम्य नाश्वासयसि पार्थिव ।।10।।

"Lord of Kings, here I am weeping and crying, and thou dost not come to console me, o King, how cruel thou art!

न शोचाम्यहमात्मानं न चान्यदपि किञ्चन ।
कथं नु भवितास्येक इति त्वां नृप रोदिमि ।।11।।

"I grieve not for me nor for anyone else. I weep only for thee, o king, how wilt thou be, all alone?

कथं नु राजंस्तृषितः क्षुधितः श्रमकर्षितः ।
सायाह्ने वृक्षमूलेषु मामपश्यन्भविष्यसि ।।12।।

"When thirsty and hungry, exhausted, at nightfall thou wilt not see me under the trees, how wilt thee feel?"

ततः सा तीव्रशोकार्ता प्रदीप्तेव च मन्युना ।
इतश्चेतश्च रुदती पर्यधावत दुःखिता ।।13।।

Then overcome with pain, like one burnt by the fire of anger, sobbing, she runs here and there.

मुहुरुत्पतते बाला मुहुः पतति विह्वला ।
मुहुरालीयते भीता मुहुः क्रोशति रोदिति ।।14।।

At times she springs forth, at times she sinks to the ground, mad with grief. At times, frightened she hides. At times she wails and sobs loudly.

अतीव शोकसंतप्ता मुहुर्निःश्वस्य विह्वला ।
उवाच भैमी निःश्वस्य रुदत्यथ पतिव्रता ।।15।।

At times, beside herself with grief, seared with extreme
pain, she sighs loudly. Weeping, the faithful daughter of
Bhima said,

यस्याभिशापाद् दुःखार्तो दुःखं विन्दति नैषधः ।
तस्य भूतस्य नो दुःखाद् दुःखमप्यधिकं भवेत् ।।16।।

"The creature by whose spell Nala had to experience
pain after pain, let this creature suffer a greater pain than
ours.

अपापचेतसं पापो य एवं कृतवान् नलम् ।
तस्माद् दुःखतरं प्राप्य जीवत्वसुखजीविकाम् ।।17।।

"Let the evil being who has reduced the innocent king
Nala to this state, live a miserable life and suffer a greater
pain than he."

एवं तु विलपन्ती सा राज्ञो भार्या महात्मनः ।
अन्वेषमाणा भर्तारं वने श्वापदसेविते ।।18।।
उन्मत्तवद् भीमसुता विलपन्ती इतस्ततः ।
हा हा राजन्निति मुहुरितश्चेतश्च धावति ।।19।।

Thus Bhima's daughter mourned and sought her lord in this forest haunted with wild beasts. Like one possessed, she runs here and there, again and again crying, "Ha, ha, King!"

तां क्रन्दमानामत्यर्थं कुररीमिव वाशतीम् ।
करुणं बहु शोचन्तीं विलपन्तीं मुहुर्मुहुः ।।20।।
सहसाभ्यागतां भैमीमभ्याशपरिवर्तिनीम् ।
जग्राहाजगरो ग्राहो महाकाव्यः क्षुधान्वितः ।।21।।

Like a bird she ceaselessly wails and her laments are heart-rending. Suddenly a hungry python with a huge body, seized her who was coming towards him.

सा ग्रस्यमाना ग्राहेण शोकेन च परिप्लुता ।
नात्मानं शोचति तथा यथा शोचति नैषधम् ।।22।।

Even while being swallowed by the python and overwhelmed with horror, she did not grieve for herself as much as she grieved for the Naishada King.

हा नाथ मामिह वने ग्रस्यमानामनाथवत् ।
ग्राहेणानेन विजने किमर्थं नानुधावसि ।।23।।

"Ah Prince, why dost thou not come rushing towards

me? I am here in this lone wood captured by this snake as
though I had no protector!

कथं भविष्यसि पुनर्मामनुसृत्य नैषध ।
कथं भवाञ्जगामाद्य मामुत्सृज्य वने प्रभो ।।24।।

"Naishadha, [when I am dead] how will it be for thee
when thee rememberest me again and again? Prabhu!
How could thee abandon me today in this jungle?

पापान्मुक्तः पुनर्लब्ध्वा बुद्धिं चेतो धनानि च ।
श्रान्तस्य ते क्षुधार्तस्य परिग्लानस्य नैषध ।
कः श्रमं राजशार्दूल नाशयिष्यति तेऽनघ ।।25।।

"Blameless Nala! When, [after this ordeal] thou hast
regained thy senses, thy consciousness and thy wealth,
thou wilt be tired, hungry and sad. Then who, my lion
among kings, will wipe away thy weariness ?"

ततः कश्चिन्मृगव्याधो विचरन् गहने वने ।
आक्रन्दमानां संश्रुत्य जवेनाभिससार ह ।।26।।
तां तु दृष्ट्वा तथा ग्रस्तामुरगेणायतेक्षणाम् ।
त्वरमाणो मृगव्याधः समभिक्रम्य वेगतः ।।27।।
मुखतः पाटयामास शस्त्रेण निशितेन च ।
निर्विचेष्टं भुजङ्गं तं विशस्य मृगजीवनः ।।28।।

मोक्षयित्वा स तां व्याधः प्रक्षाल्य सलिलेन ह ।
समाश्वास्य कृताहारामथ पप्रच्छ भारत ।।29।।

A hunter roaming through the deep forest, heard her bewailing and approached rapidly. Seeing a woman caught by that snake, he came running. With a sharp weapon he tore the head of the snake. Then he freed Damayanti, who washed her body with water. He gave her many reassurances and after she had eaten something, he asked her,

कस्य त्वं मृगशावाक्षि कथं चाभ्यागता वनम् ।
कथं चेदं महत् कृच्छ्रं प्राप्तवत्यसि भाविनि ।।30।।

"Who is thy husband, o thou with the fawn's eyes? How camest thee in this jungle? And how hast thee been reduced to this miserable state, noble lady?"

दमयन्ती तथा तेन पृच्छ्यमाना विशाम्पते ।
सर्वमेतद् यथावृत्तमाचचक्षेऽस्य भारत ।।31।।

O, king Yudhishthira, [said Brihadashva] then Damayanti asked by him recounted all that had befallen her.

तामर्धवस्त्रसंवीतां पीनश्रोणिपयोधराम् ।
सुकुमारानवद्याङ्गीं पूर्णचन्द्रनिभाननाम् ।।32।।
अरालपक्ष्मनयनां तथा मधुरभाषिणीम् ।
लक्षयित्वा मृगव्याधः कामस्य वशमीयिवान् ।।33।।

Seeing her with half a cloth, of full hips and breasts,
her whose body was without a blemish, whose face was
glowing like the full moon, whose eyes were with curving
lashes, and whose voice was melodious, the hunter fell to
desire.

तामेवं श्लक्ष्णया वाचा लुब्धको मृदुपूर्वया ।
सान्त्वयामास कामार्तस्तदबुध्यत भाविनी ।।38।।

With sweet and tender words, this greedy man,
tormented by lust, tried to console her. The noble lady
understood.

दमयन्त्यपि तं दुष्टमुपलभ्य पतिव्रता ।
तीव्ररोपसमाविष्टा प्रजज्वालेव मन्युना ।।35।।

The faithful Damayanti perceived his evil intention and
filled with a fierce anger burnt as it were with the fire of
wrath.

स तु पापमतिः क्षुद्र प्रधर्षयितुमातुरः ।
दुर्धर्षां तर्कयामास दीप्तामग्निशिखामिव ।।36।।

Although this vile and wicked hunter was intending to take her by force, he did hesitate to touch her, bright as a flame, invincible.

दमयन्ती तु दुःखार्ता पतिराज्यविनाकृता ।
अतीतवाक्पथे काले शशापैनं रुषन्विता ।।37।।

But Damayanti, albeit so desolate, abandoned by her lord, stripped of her kingdom, cursed him angrily, as the time for supplication was over.

यद्यहं नैषधादन्यं मनसापि न चिन्तये ।
तथायं पततां क्षुद्रो पुरासुमृर्गजीवनः ।।38।।

"If it is true that I have never given a thought to any man save the Naishadha king, then may this vile hunter fall dead!"

उक्तमात्रे तु वचने तथा स मृगजीवनः ।
व्यसुः पपात मेदिन्यामग्निदग्ध इव दुमः ।।39।।

Hardly had she spoken when the hunter fell to earth, stone dead, like a tree burned by a lightening bolt.

Leaving that place and oppressed by grief, the queen went deeper still into the forest. Whom could she ask for tidings of her lord? When evening fell, she saw a tiger looking for its prey. She approached him:

chap 64

अरण्यराडयं श्रीमांश्चतुर्दर्ष्ट्रो महाहनुः । ।31। ।
शार्दूलोऽभिमुखोऽभ्येति व्रजाम्येनमशङ्किता ।
भवान् मृगाणामधिपस्त्वमस्मिन् कानने प्रभुः । ।32। ।

"Here comes the king of the forest. His great jaws armed with four-fold fangs. A tiger is approaching and stands face to face on my path. I shall go to him fearlessly: 'Sir, thou art the chief of the beasts and the master of this forest.

विदर्भराजतनयां दमयन्तीति विद्धि माम् ।
निषधाधिपतेर्भार्या नलस्यामित्रघातिनः । ।33। ।

'Know me to be Damayanti, the daughter of the king of Vidarbha, the wife of the king of Nishadha, the subduer of his foes.

पतिमन्वेषतीमेकां कृपणां शोककर्शिताम् ।
आश्वासय मृगेन्द्रेह यदि दृष्टस्त्वया नलः ॥ 34 ॥

'I am alone in this jungle searching for my husband, miserable, sorrow-stricken, o Lord of the beasts, if thou hast seen Nala, comfort me.

अथवा त्वं वनपते नलं यदि न शंससि ।
मां खादय मृगश्रेष्ठ दुःखादस्माद् विमोचय ॥ 35 ॥

'But if thou canst not speak about him, then king of the forest, devour me, savage lord, and set me free from this woe.'

श्रुत्वारण्ये विलपितं न मामाश्वासयत्ययम् ।
यात्येतां स्वादुसलिलामापगां सागरंहामाम् ॥ 36 ॥

"This tiger has heard me crying yet he does not comfort me. He directs his steps towards the river, full of sweet water, flowing towards the ocean."

Then Damayanti saw a great mountain that reared its crest high into the heavens. She asked the mountain if it had seen her husband. But the mountain did not answer a word.

For three days and nights she wandered, her feet leading her to the North. At last she saw stretched in front of her a beautiful grove inhabited by holy men, clad with bark. They lived in contemplation and had mastered their senses. Some lived only on water or air, some lived only on the leaves fallen from the trees. A ring of huts formed an ashram around which one could see different kinds of animals grazing peacefully. They welcomed Damayanti and asked her who she was. She told the holy men the tale of her life. The seers told her,

chap 64 (contd)

उदर्कस्तव कल्याणि कल्याणो भविता शुभे ।
वयं पश्याम तपसा क्षिप्रं द्रक्ष्यसि नैषधम् ।।92।।

"Fair lady, your future will be bright. We can see by the power of our tapasya. Soon you will behold Naishadha.

निषधानामधिपतिं नलं रिपुनिपातिनम् ।
भैमि धर्मभृतां श्रेष्ठं द्रक्ष्यसे विगतज्वरम् ।।93।।

"O! daughter of Bhima, thou wilt see Nala again, thou wilt see the king of the Nishadhas, the terror of his foes, the best among those firm in dharma, and he will be freed from troubles.

विमुक्तं सर्वपापेभ्यः सर्वरत्नसमन्वितम् ।
तदेव नगरं श्रेष्ठं प्रशासतमरिंदमम् ।।94
द्विपतां भयकर्तारं सुहृदां शोकनाशनम् ।
पतिं द्रक्ष्यसि कल्याणि कल्याणाभिजनं नृपम् ।।95।।

"Thou wilt see your husband purged of all sins and covered with gems, thou wilt see him the subduer of his foes, ruling again over the same city, giving fear to enemies and wiping out the pain of his friends, o fair lady, thou wilt see this king of a noble descent."

एवमुक्त्वा नलस्येष्टां महिषीं पार्थिवात्मजाम् ।
अन्तर्हितास्तापसास्ते साग्निहोत्राश्रमास्तथा ।।96।।

Having said these words to the dear queen of Nala, daughter of a king, these ascetics disappeared from sight along with the ashram and holy fires.

सा दृष्ट्वा महदाश्चर्यं विस्मिता ह्यभवत् तदा ।
दमयन्त्यनवद्याङ्गी वीरसेननृपस्नुषा ।।97।।

Then seeing this great wonder Damayanti of perfect beauty, daughter-in-law of king Viresena, was amazed.

किं नु स्वप्नो मया दृष्टः कोऽयं विधिरिहाभवत् ।
क्व नु ते तापसाः सर्वे क्व तदाश्रममण्डलम् । ।98। ।

"Is it a dream that I saw? What kind of miracle took place? Where are all those ascetics? Where is the ashram?

क्व सा पुण्यजला रम्या नदी द्विजनिषेविता ।
क्व नु ह नगा हृद्याः फलपुष्पोपशोभिताः । ।99। ।

"Where is that river with clear water inhabited by birds? Where are the charming trees covered with flowers and fruits?"

Damayanti continued her journey to the North searching for her husband. One day, she met a company of merchants, going to the land of Subahu, King of the Chedis. The merchants and the queen journeyed several days together until they came to a large lake. They halted and camped close to its waters. The same night a herd of elephants came there to drink, and as the camp blocked their path they rushed through it, trampling it under and goring with their tusks all who came in their way. Many merchants perished and some of those who escaped accused Damayanti of being an evil spirit and the cause of their woes. Fearing for her life the queen left them and fled into the forest.

chap 65

अशोचत् तत्र वैदर्भी किं नु मे दुष्कृतं कृतम् ।
योऽपि मे निर्जनेऽरण्ये सम्प्राप्तोऽयं जनार्णवः ।।37।।
स हतो हस्तियूथेन मन्दभग्यान्ममैव तत् ।
प्राप्तव्यं सुचिरं दुःखं नूनमद्यापि वै मया ।।38।।

The princess of Vidarbha felt very sad and reflected, "What crime have I committed, that in this desolate forest I came across a group of people as large as the sea and they were killed by a herd of elephants? All this has been brought about by my ill luck. No doubt sorrow after sorrow I will have to bear.

नाप्राप्तकालो म्रियते श्रुतं वृद्धानुशासनम् ।
या नाहमद्य मृदिता हस्तियूथेन दुःखिता ।।39।।

"None dies before his time, this is the lore of ancient sages. This is why — even though I am so sad that I would be glad to die — I was not trampled upon by the elephants.

न ह्यदैवकृतं किंचिन्नराणामिह विद्यते ।
न च मे बालभावेऽपि किंचित् पापकृतं कृतम् ।।40
कर्मणा मनसा बालभावेऽपि वाचा यदिदं दुःखमागतम् ।

"Nothing, good or bad, happens to man unless by destiny. From my childhood I have not wrought any wrong in thought, word or deed which could bring me such grief.

मन्ये स्वयंवरकृते लोकपालाः समागताः । ।41। ।
प्रख्याता मया तत्र नलस्यार्थाय देवताः ।
नूनं तेषां प्रभावेण वियोगं प्राप्तवत्यहम् । ।42। ।
एवमादीनि दुःखार्ता सा विलप्य वराङ्गना ।
प्रलापानि तदा तानि दमयन्ती पतिव्रता । ।43। ।

"I think for the sake of Nala I rejected the gods who had come to my swayamvara. It is due to their influence that today I am experiencing the pain of separation." Thus the faithful and fair Damayanti poured out her grief.

हतशेषैः सह तदा ब्राह्मणैर्वेदपारगैः ।
अगच्छद् राजशार्दूल चन्द्रलेखेव शारदी । ।44। ।
गच्छन्ती साचिराद् बाला पुरमासादयन्महत् ।
सायास्ने चेदिराजस्य सुबाहोः सत्यदर्शिनः । ।45। ।

O Yudhishthira! [said Brihadashva] Then with certain brahmins saved from the massacre — men who had read the Vedas — she travelled, beautiful and sad like the moon crescent in autumn, and soon one evening she arrived in the capital of the King of Chedis, the just Subahu.

अथ वस्त्रार्धसंवीता प्रविवेश पुरोत्तमम् ।
तां विह्वलां कृशां दीनां मुक्तकेशीममार्जिताम् ॥46॥

Clad with half a garment she entered the great city. She was mad with grief, emaciated and weak, her hair was loose, and she was unwashed.

उन्मत्तामिव गच्छन्तीं ददृशुः पुरवासिनः ।
प्रविशन्तीं तु तां दृष्ट्वा चेदिराजपुरीं तदा ॥47॥
अनुजग्मुस्तत्र बाला ग्रामिपुत्राः कुतूहलात् ।
सा तैः परिवृतागच्छत् समीपं राजवेश्मनः ॥48॥

The inhabitants of the city saw her walking like a mad woman. At that time village children saw her enter the capital and followed her with curiosity. Surrounded by them she approached the royal palace.

The queen mother of the Chedis was touched by the great beauty and nobility of Damayanti. She advised her daughter, Sunanda, to take her as her companion. Sunanda looked at Damayanti and loved her instantly. Damayanti made it very clear that the queens must protect her as she was the faithful wife of a man who, for no fault of his own, had left her. She would not bear to be wooed by any man.

* * *

Several years passed.

The king Bhima sent emissaries everywhere to try and find a trace of Damayanti and Nala. One of them, a brahmin named Sudeva one day arrived in the city of the Chedi king and recognized Damayanti by the tiny mole between her eyebrows. A little later, Damayanti escorted by a strong band of horsemen returned to Vidarbha with Sudeva.

Let us now go back to the story as retold by Sister Nivedita:

... Once more Damayanti was dwelling — but now with her children by her side — in her father's house. For Bhima had sent out messengers in all directions to seek for her, and by them had she been found and brought back to her own people: But always she wore but half a veil, never would she use ornaments, and even she waited sorrowfully for the coming again of her husband, Nala. For in all this time he had never been heard of.

Now it had happened to Nala that on finally leaving Damayanti he saw a mighty forest fire, and from its midst he heard the voice of some creature crying, "Come to my aid, O mighty Nala!"

Saying, "Fear not!" the King stepped at once within the circle of fire, and beheld an enormous snake lying there coiled up.

And the snake spoke, saying, "I have been cursed, O King, to remain here, unable to move, till one named Nala carry me hence. And only on that spot to which he shall carry me can I be made free from this curse. And now, O Nala, if thou wilt lift me in thy hands, I shall be thy friend and do to thee great good. Moreover, there is no snake equal unto me. I can make myself small and light in thy hands. I beseech thee to lift me and let us go hence!"

Then that great snake made himself as small as the human thumb, and taking him in his hands, Nala carried him to a place outside the fire. But as he was about to place him on the ground, the snake bit him, and Nala perceived that as he was bitten, his form had been changed.

And the snake spoke, saying, "Nala, be comforted! I have deprived thee of thy beauty, that none may recognise thee. And he who has wronged and betrayed thee shall dwell in thee from this time in uttermost torture. Henceforth art thou in peace, and that evil one in torment from my venom. But go thou now to Ayodhya, and present thyself before the king there, who is skilled in gambling. Offer him thy services as a charioteer. Give to him thy skill with horses, in exchange for his knowledge of dice. When thou dost understand the dice, thy wife and children will be thine once more. And finally, O King, when thou desirest to regain thy proper form, think of me and wear these garments." And saying these words that lord of Nagas gave unto Nala two pieces of enchanted clothing, and immediately became invisible.

And Nala made his way to Ayodhya, and entered the service of Rituparna the King, receiving great honour as the Master of the Horse. And all the stables and their attendants were placed under him; for Rituparna desired nothing so much as that his steeds should be fleet.

But night after night the fellow officers of the charioteer — who was known in the palace of Ayodhya as Vahuka — would hear him alone, groaning and weeping, and listening they distinctly heard the words: "Alas! where layeth she now her head, a-hungered and a-thirst, helpless and worn with toil, thinking ever of him who was unworthy? Where dwelleth she now? On whose bidding doth she wait?" And once, when they begged him to tell them who it was that he thus lamented, he told them in veiled words his whole story. "A certain person," he said, "had a beautiful wife, but little sense. The wretch was false. He kept not his promises. Fate came upon him, and they were separated. Without her, he wandered ever to and fro oppressed with woe, and now, burning with grief, he resteth not by day nor night. At last he has found a refuge, but each hour that passes only reminds him of her. When calamity had overtaken this man, his wife followed him into the wild woods. He repaid her by deserting her there! Abandoned by him, lost in the forest, fainting with hunger and thirst, ever exposed to the perils of the wilderness, her very life was put by him in danger. Yea, my friends, it was by him — by him that she was thus deserted, by him, that very man, so foolish and ill-fated, that she was left thus alone in the great and terrible forest, surrounded on every side by beasts of prey — by him, by him!"

With his mind dwelling thus on Damayanti, did Vahuka the charioteer live in the palace of Rituparna. And Damayanti, sheltered once more in her father's house, had one thought, and one only, and that was the possibility of recovering Nala. Now it was the custom amongst the Vidarbhas to send out Brahmins periodically, who, bearing the King's orders, wandered from town to town and from country to country, telling stories to the people from the holy books, and giving religious instruction wherever it was needed. It had indeed been by the aid of these strolling teachers that Damayanti herself had been discovered, when she was acting as lady-in-waiting to a foreign princess. Now, therefore, it was decided that she should give them their directions, and try by their means to trace out her long-lost husband. They came to her therefore for instructions, and she gave them a song which they were to sing in all the assemblies that they should come to in every realm.

"Whither, beloved Gambler, whither art thou gone,
Cutting off one half my veil,
Abandoning me, thy devoted wife,
Asleep in the forest?

Ever do I await thee,
As thou wouldst desire me,
Wearing but half a veil,
Enwrapt in sorrow.

Relent, O King! O Hero!
Relent and return thee,
To her who weepeth incessantly
For thy departure!"

"Crying thus, add to the part your own words," she said to the Brahmins, "that his pity be awakened. Fanned by the wind, the fire consumeth the forest!"

Again —

"Surely a wife should be protected
And maintained by her husband.
Strange that, noble as thou art,
Thou neglectest both these duties!

Wise thou wast, and famous,
High-born and full of kindness.
Why didst thou then deal to me this blow?
Alas, the fault was mine!
My good fortune had departed from me!

Yet even so, thou greatest, thou noblest
Amongst men, even so, have pity,
Be merciful to me!"

"If, after ye have sung in this wise," said Damayanti to the Brahmins, "any should chance to speak with you, oh, bring me word of him! I must know who he is, and where he dwelleth. But take ye great heed that none may guess the words ye speak to be at my bidding, nor that ye will afterwards return to me. And do not fail, I beseech ye, to seek out all that is to be known regarding that man who shall answer to your song!"

Having received these orders, the Brahmins set out in all directions to do the bidding of Damayanti. And their quest led them far and near, through cities and villages, into strange kingdoms, amongst forests, hermitages, and monasteries, and from one camp of roving cowherds to another. And wherever they went they sang the songs and played the part that Damayanti had laid upon them, seeking in every place, if by any means they might bring back to her news of Nala.

And when a long time had passed away, one of these Brahmins returned to Damayanti, and said to her, "O Damayanti, seeking Nala, the king of the Nishadas, I came to the city of Ayodhya, and appeared before Rituparna. But though I repeatedly sang thy songs, neither that King nor any of his courtiers answered anything. Then, when I had been dismissed by the monarch, I was accosted by one of his servants, Vahuka the charioteer. And Vahuka is of uncomely[1] looks and figure, and possessed of very short arms. But he is skilful in the management of horses, and is also acquainted with the art of cookery.

"And this Vahuka, with many sighs and some tears, came up to me and asked about my welfare. And then he said, 'She should not be angry with one whose garment was carried off by birds, when he was trying to procure food for both! The honour of a woman is its own best guard. Let her not be angered against one who is consumed with grief. Noble women are ever faithful, ever true to their own lords, and whether treated well or ill, they will forgive one who has lost all he loved!' Hearing this, O Princess, I hastened back to tell thee. Do now what seemeth best unto thyself."

Words cannot describe the joy of Damayanti as she heard this news. She knew now where Nala was, and the task with which he was entrusted. It lay only with her woman's wit to find some means of bringing him to her father's house. Having pondered long and carefully over the matter, she went to her mother, and in her presence sent for the same confidential servant — a kind of chaplain to the royal household —who had found

---

1. uncomely = ugly

herself and brought her back from exile to the city of the Vidarbhas. Having her mother's full sanction, but keeping the matter secret from Bhima, Damayanti turned to this Brahmin, Sudeva, and said, "Go straight as a bird, Sudeva, to the city of Ayodhya and tell Rituparna the King that Bhima's daughter, Damayanti, will once more hold a Swayamvara. Kings and princes from all parts are coming to it. Knowing not whether the heroic Nala lives or not, it is decided that she is again to choose a husband. Tomorrow at sunrise, say thou, when thou seest him, the ceremony will take place." And Sudeva, bowing before the Queen-mother and her daughter, left the royal presence, and proceeded to Ayodhya.

When Rituparna heard the news, he sent immediately for Vahuka, the charioteer. If he desired in one day to reach the city of the Vidarbhas, there was only one driver in the world who could enable him to do so. "Exert thyself, O Vahuka!" he exclaimed. "Damayanti, daughter of Bhima, holds tomorrow a second Swayamvara, and I desire to reach the city this very day!"

Hearing these words Nala felt as if his heart would break. "What!" he thought to himself, "is this the madness of sorrow? Or is it perhaps a punishment for me? Ah, cruel is this deed that she would do! It may be that, urged by my own folly, the stainless Princess cares for me no longer. Yet I cannot believe that she, my wife, and the mother of my children, could possibly dream of wedding any other. In any case, however, there is but one thing to be done. By going there I shall do the will of Rituparna, and also satisfy myself." Having thus reflected, Vahuka answered the King, saying, "O Monarch, I bow to thy behest.[1] Thou shalt reach the city of the Vidarbhas in a single day."

Wonderful and eventful was the driving of Vahuka the charioteer that day. Never had Rituparna, or the servant who attended him, seen such skill. The servant indeed remembered, as he watched it, the fame of Nala. But he turned his eyes upon the driver, and seeing his want of beauty, decided that this could hardly be he, even though he should be disguised and living as a servant, in consequence of misfortune. Every now and then the chariot would rise into the sky, and course along with the fleetness of the wind. Like a bird would it cross rivers and mountains, woods and lakes. In a few seconds it would speed over as many miles. And Rituparna knew not how to express his delight in the skill of his charioteer. Words could not speak his anxiety to reach the city of the Vidarbhas before nightfall; and more and more, as the hours went on, did he become convinced that only with the help of Vahuka was this possible. But about noon the two became involved in a dispute about the number of leaves and fruits on a certain tree. Rituparna, who was

---

1. behest = command

a great mathematician, said there were so many, and his officer insisted on stopping the car, cutting down the tree, and counting, to see if the King's words were true! Rituparna was in despair. He could not go on without Vahuka, and Vahuka was intent on verifying the numbers. However, the charioteer was sufficiently amazed and respectful to the King's knowledge when he had counted the fruits and found them to be correct. Then, in order to coax him onwards, Rituparna said, "Come on, Vahuka, and in exchange for thy knowledge of horses, I will give thee my knowledge of dice. For I understand every secret of the gaming table." This was the very moment for which Nala had waited and served so long! However, he preserved his composure, and immediately the King imparted to him his knowledge. And lo! As he did so, Kali, the spirit of darkness, came forth, invisible to others, from within Nala, and he felt himself suddenly to be released from all weakness and blindness, and to have again all his old time energy and power. And radiant with renewal of strength, the charioteer mounted once more on the chariot, and taking the reins in his hands, drove swiftly to the city of the Vidarbhas.

As Rituparna, towards evening, entered the city, the sound of the driving of his chariot fell on the ears of Damayanti in the palace, and she remembered, with a thrill, the touch of Nala on a horse's reins. But, mounting to one of the terraces, she looked out, and could see only one who drove like Nala, but none who had his face and form. "Ah!" she sighed, "if he does not come to me today, tomorrow I enter the funeral fire! I can bear no longer this life of sorrow!"

The King of Ayodhya meanwhile, hastening to call on Bhima, began to think there must have been some mistake. He saw no other kings and princes with their chariots. He heard no word of any Swayamvara. He therefore said that he had come merely to pay his respects. This, thought the King of the Vidarbhas, was a little strange. A man would not usually come so far and in such hot haste, in a single day, merely for a passing visit of courtesy. However, feeling sure that the reason would reveal itself later, he proceeded to offer Rituparna the attentions due to his rank and importance.

Nala, however, had no eyes for anything about him. Buried in thought, he gave orders for the disposal of the horses, and having seen them duly carried out, sat down with arms folded and head bent. At the sound of a woman's voice he looked up. A maid sent from within the palace was asking him, in the name of Damayanti, why and for what purpose had he and Rituparna come. "We came," answered the charioteer bitterly, "because the King heard that the Princess of the Vidarbhas would for a second time hold a Swayamvara!" "And who art thou?"

again asked the maiden. "Who art thou? And who yon servant yonder? Might either of ye by chance have heard aught of Nala? It may even be that thou knowest whither King Nala is gone!"

"Nay, nay!" answered Vahuka. "That King in his calamity wanders about the world, disguised, and despoiled even of his beauty. Nala's self only knoweth Nala, and she also that is his second self. Nala never discovereth his secret to any!"

"And yet," replied the maid, "we sent a Brahmin to Ayodhya, and when he sang —

'Ah, beloved Gambler, whither art thou gone,
Taking with thee half my veil,
And leaving me, who loved thee,
Sleeping in the woods?
Speak thou, great King, the words I long to hear,
For I who am without stain pant to hear them!'

when he sang thus, thou didst make some reply. Repeat thy words now, I beseech thee. My mistress longeth again to hear those words!"

At this Nala answered in a voice half choked: "She ought not to be angry with one whose garment was carried off by birds, when he was trying to procure food for both! The honour of a woman is its own best guard. Let her not be

angered against one who is consumed with grief. Noble
women are ever faithful, ever true to their own lords, and,
whether treated well or ill, they will forgive one who is
deprived of every joy!" As he ended, the King could no
longer restrain himself, but burying his head in his arms,
gave way to his sorrow; and the girl, seeing this, stole away
silently to tell all to the Princess.

News was brought also to Damayanti of the greatness
and power of Rituparna's charioteer. It was told her how
on coming to a low doorway he would not stoop down, but
the passage itself would grow higher in his presence, that
he might easily enter it. Vessels at his will filled themselves
with water. He needed not to strike to obtain fire, for on
holding a handful of grass in the sun, it would of its own
accord burst into flame in his hand. Hearing these and
other things, Darnayanti became sure that the charioteer
Vahuka was no other than Nala, her husband. Yet, that
she might put him to one more test, she sent her maid,
with her two children, to wander near him. On seeing
them, Nala took them into his arms and embraced them,
with tears. Then, realising how strange this must seem,
he turned to the waiting-woman and said apologetically
— "They are so like my own! But do not thou, maiden,
come this way again. We are strangers here from a far
land. We are unknown, and I would fain[1] be alone."

---

1. fain = prefer

And now, having heard this, Damayanti could wait no longer, but sent for the permission of her father and mother, and had Nala brought to her own apartments. Coming thus into her presence, and seeing her clad just as he had left her, wearing only half her veil, the seeming charioteer was shaken with grief. And Damayanti, feeling sure that he was Nala, and seeing him as a servant, whose wont it was to be a king, could scarcely restrain her tears. But she composed herself, and said quietly, "Well, Vahuka, did you ever hear of a good man who went away and left a devoted wife, sleeping alone, in the forest? Ah, what was the fault that Nala found in me, that he should so have left me, helpless and alone? Did I not choose him once in preference to the very gods themselves? And did he not, in their presence, and in that of the fire, take me by the hand, and say, 'Verily, I shall be ever thine'? Where was that promise, do you think, when he left me thus?"

And Nala answered, "In truth, it was not my fault. It was the act of Kali, who hath now left me, and for that only, have I come hither! But, Damayanti, was there ever a true woman who, like thee, could choose a second husband? At this moment have the messengers of thy father gone out over the whole world, crying, 'Bhima's daughter will choose again a husband who shall be worthy of her.' For this it is that Rituparna is come hither!"

Then Damayanti, trembling and frighted, folded her hands before Nala, and said, "O dear and blessed Lord, suspect me not of evil! This was but my scheme to bring thee hither. Excepting thee, there was none in the whole world who could drive here quickly enough. Let the gods before whom I chose thee, let the sun and the moon and the air, tell thee truly that every thought of mine has been for thee!" And at the words, flowers fell from the sky, and a voice said, "Verily Damayanti is full of faith and honour! Damayanti is without stain!"

Then was the heart of Nala at peace within him. And he remembered his change of form, and drawing forth the enchanted garments, he put them on, keeping his mind fixed on the great Naga. And when Damayanri saw Nala again in his own form, she made salutation to him as her husband, and began to weep. Then were their children brought to them, and the Queen-mother gave her blessing, and hour after hour passed in recounting the sorrows of their separation.

The next day were Nala and Damayanti received together in royal audience by Bhima. And in due time, Kali being now gone out from him, Nala made his way to his own kingdom of the Nishadas and recovered his throne, and then, returning for his Queen, Damayanti, and their children, he took them all back to their own home, and they lived there happily together ever after.

Notes

I. Vyasa

मुनीनामप्यहं व्यासः : "Of the Munis I am Vyasa" (Bhagavad Gita 10.37)

First among the Munis: such was the place given to the Rishi Vyasa by ancient India.

The name of Vyasa is common to many old authors and compilers, but it is especially applied to Veda-Vyasa or Krishna Dvaipayana. He was the son of Rishi Parashara and Satyavati. From his complexion (dark) he received the name Krishna, and from his birthplace (an island, *dvip*, in the Yamuna), the name Dvaipayana. He was a Rishi himself and is traditionally cited as the author of the Mahabharata and many other works, but he is best known as the compiler of the Vedas (Veda-Vyasa means "the one who arranged the Vedas").

No one knows exactly how many verses the Mahabharata originally contained. Some speak of 4400 verses, some others of 8800, still some others of 26400. What is certain is that over a period of time, the number of verses increased tremendously, many times its original size, and the epic as it is known today (110000 shlokas —

or, as some people prefer to count, 220000 lines) contains a great number of later interpolations. Dayananda Saraswati remarked that it resembles a camel to whose burden people kept adding.[1] Thus the epic is seven-fold greater in bulk than the Iliad and Odyssey taken together.

Vyasa is said to have taught the poem to one of his pupils, Vaishampayana. Vaishampayana, in his turn, recited the epic to Janamejaya, grand-son of Abhimanyu.

It would be hazardous to assign a date to Vyasa's birth or to the composing of the Mahabharata. According to Indian tradition the events described in the epic, the great war fought between the Kauravas and the Pandavas, took place around 3100 BC (the beginning of the Kali age, which is mentioned in the epic: *praaptam kaliyugam viddhi*). But the date at which the epic was composed varies considerably according to the critics. What can be said with certainty is that the Mahabharata belongs to the second period of the ancient history of India. After the Vedic age, also called the age of intuition, this period begins with the birth of the Buddha to the fall of the Mauryan empire. It marks the transition from the age of intuition to the age of reason. It is during that period that the great epic literature, the great philosophical systems, the codes of ethics, the codes of statecraft as well as the sciences and arts began to develop.

---

1. Dayananda Saraswati, *Satyarthaprakash*.

II. NALOPAKHYANAM

The story of Nala is said to be very ancient. It seems that the name of Nala, king of Nishada, goes back to Vedic antiquity. As Edwin Arnold (a poet who gave a rendition of Nalopakhyanam in verse) said: "I believe certain portions of the mighty poem which here appear, and many other episodes, to be of far greater antiquity than has been ascribed to the Mahabharata generally. Doubtless the 'two hundred and twenty thousand lines' of the entire compilation contain in many places little and large additions and corrections... and he who ever so slightly explores this poetical ocean will, indeed, perceive defects, excrescences, differences, and breaks of artistic style or structure. But in the simpler and nobler sections the Sanskrit verse (ofttimes as musical and highly wrought as Homer's own Greek) bears, as I think, testimony... to an origin anterior to writing, anterior to Puranic theology, anterior to Homer, perhaps even to Moses."

This story was told and retold many times after the composing of the original Mahabharata. M. Krishnamachariar in his *History of Classical Sanskrit Literature* mentions at least thirteen poems and four dramas (in Sanskrit alone) based on the story. A poem called Nalodaya is sometimes attributed to Kalidasa.

Damayanti, painting by Bengali artist
Nandalal Bose (detail)

III. Vyasa's art

It has been said that Vyasa was the most masculine of writers. What is meant by this statement is that tendencies usually associated, rightly or wrongly, with the feminine temperament such as love of ornament, great emotionalism, excessive sensitiveness to form and beauty, a certain lack of self-restraint and the primacy of imagination over reason, are absent from Vyasa's genius. His style is unadorned, we do not find in it many similes or metaphors. On the contrary, it is marked by an austere self-restraint. Vyasa's characteristics are the strength of his mind, the grandeur of his intellect. His art is the expression of a forceful mind in which the idea is sufficient to itself. He does not write to create something beautiful, but because he has certain ideas to impart, certain events to describe, certain characters to portray. He has an image of these in his mind and his business is to find a precise expression for it.

It could be rightly assumed that strength and a fine austerity are the two tests that give us safe guidance through the huge body of the Mahabharata. Where these two exist together, we can be sure that this is Vyasa's hand and not that of some interpolator.

And paradoxically, nowhere is this restrained art more visible than when he handles the miraculous, particularly

in the story of Nala and Damayanti. As Sri Aurobindo
says:

> *In such surroundings wonders might seem natural*
> *and deities as in Arcadia might peep from under*
> *every tree. Nala's messengers to Damayanti are a*
> *troop of golden-winged swans that speak with a*
> *human voice; he is intercepted on his way by gods*
> *who make him their envoy to a mortal maiden; he*
> *receives from them gifts more than human, fire and*
> *water come to him at his bidding and flowers bloom*
> *in his hands; in his downfall the dice become birds*
> *who fly away with his remaining garment; when he*
> *wishes to cut in half the robe of Damayanti, a sword*
> *came ready to his hand in the desolate cabin; he meets*
> *the Serpent-King in the ring of fire and is turned by*
> *him into the deformed charioteer, Bahuka; the tiger*
> *in the forest turns away from Damayanti without*
> *injuring her and the lustful hunter falls consumed*
> *by the power of offended chastity. The destruction of*
> *the caravan by wild elephants, the mighty driving of*
> *Nala, the counting of the leaves or the cleaving of the*
> *Vibhitaka tree; every incident almost is full of that*
> *sense of beauty and wonder which were awakened*
> *in Vyasa by his early surroundings. We ask whether*
> *this beautiful fairy-tale is the work of that stern and*
> *high poet with whom the actualities of life were*

everything and the flights of fancy counted for so little. Yet, if we look carefully, we shall see in the Nala abundant proof of the severe touch of Vyasa, just as in his share of the Mahabharata fleeting touches of wonder and strangeness, gone as soon as glimpsed, evidence a love of the supernatural, severely bitted and reined in. Especially do we see the poet of the Mahabharata in the artistic vigilance which limits each supernatural incident to a few light strokes, to the exact place and no other where it is wanted and the exact amount and no more than is necessary. (It is this sparing economy of touch almost unequalled in its beauty of just rejection, which makes the poem an epic instead of a fairy-tale in verse). There is, for instance, the incident of the swans; we all know to what prolixities of pathos and bathos vernacular poets like the Gujarati Premanand[1] have enlarged this feature of the story. But Vyasa introduced it to give a certain touch of beauty and strangeness and that touch once imparted, the swans disappear from the scene; for his fine taste felt that to prolong the incident by one touch more would have been to lower the form and run the risk of raising a smile.[2]

---

1. Premanand: a Gujarati poet, 1636-1734.
2. Sri Aurobindo, Centenary Edition, Vol III (Pondicherry: Sri Aurobindo Ashram, 1972), p. 153.

Vyasa's descriptions of nature are very few. And when he does describe a natural scene, he is more interested in rendering its essence and its atmosphere, clearly and briefly. But these descriptions of nature are rare and, as Sri Aurobindo says,

> *He is far more in his element in the expression of the feelings, of the joy and sorrow that makes this life of men; his description of emotion far excels his description of things.*
> *When he says of Damayanti:*

विललाप सुदुःखिता ।
भर्तृशोकपरिताङ्गी शिलातलमथाश्रिता [1]

> *In grief she wailed*
> *Erect upon a cliff, her body aching*
> *With sorrow for her husband,*
> *the clear figure of the abandoned woman lamenting on the cliff seizes indeed the imagination, but it has a lesser inspiration than the single puissant and convincing epithet bhartrsokaparitangi, her whole body affected with grief for her husband. Damayanti's longer laments are also of the finest sweetness and strength; there is a rushing flow of*

---
1. The Mahabharata, Vanaparva, 64.12.

stately and sorrowful verse, the wailing of a regal grief; then as some more exquisite pain, some more piercing gust of passion traverses the heart of the mourner, golden felicities of sorrow leap out on the imagination like lightning in their swift clear greatness.

हा वीर नल नामाहं नष्टा किल तवानघ ।
अस्यामटव्यां घोरायां किं मां न प्रतिभाषसे । ।[1]

Still more strong, simple and perfect is the grief of Damayanti when she wakes to find herself alone in that desolate cabin. The restraint of phrase is perfect, the verse is clear, equable and unadorned, yet hardly has Valmiki himself written a truer utterance of emotion than this:

हा नाथ हा महाराज हा स्वामिन्किं जहासि माम् ।
हा हतास्मि विनष्टास्मि भीतास्मि विजने वने । ।
ननु नाम महाराज धर्मज्ञः सत्यवागसि ।
कथमुक्त्वा तथा सत्यं सुप्तामुत्सृज्य मां गतः ।
पर्याप्तः परिहासोऽयमेतावान्पुरुषर्षभ ।
भीताहमतिदुर्धर्ष दर्शयात्मानमीश्वर । ।
दृश्यसे दृश्यसे राजन्नेष दृष्टोऽसि नैषध ।

1. The Mahabharata, Vanaparva, 64.19. "Ah Nala, my pure Lord! I am destroyed! Why dost thou not answer thy wife in this terrible forest?"

आवार्य गुल्मैरात्मानं किं मां न प्रतिभाषसे । ।
नृशंस बत राजेन्द्र यन्मामेवङ्गतामिह ।
विलपन्तीं समागम्य नाश्वासयसि पार्थिव । ।
न शोचाम्यहमात्मानं न चान्यदपि किञ्चन ।
कथं नु भवितास्येक इति त्वां नृप रोदिमि । ।
कथं नु राजंस्तृषितः क्षुधितः श्रमकर्षितः ।
सायाह्ने वृक्षमूलेषु मामपश्यन्नभविष्यसि । । [1]

"Ah my lord! Ah my king! Ah my husband! Why hast thou forsaken me? Alas, I am slain, I am undone, I am afraid in the lonely forest. Surely, O king, thou wert good and truthful, how then having sworn to me so, hast thou abandoned me in my sleep and fled? Long enough hast thou carried this jest of thine, O lion of men, I am frightened, O unconquerable; show thyself, my lord and prince. I see thee! I see thee! Thou art seen, O lord of the Nishadas, covering thyself there with the bushes; why dost thou not speak to me? Cruel king! that thou dost not come to me thus terrified here and wailing and comfort me! It is not for myself I grieve nor for aught else; it is for thee I weep thinking what will become of thee left all alone. How wilt thou fare under some tree at evening, hungry and thirsty and

---

1. The Mahabharata, Vanaparva, 63, 3,4,8-12.

weary, not beholding me, O my king?"
The whole of this passage with its first pang of terror
and the exquisite anticlimax, "I am slain, I am
undone, I am afraid in the desert wood", passing
quietly into sorrowful reproach, the despairing and
pathetic attempt to delude herself by thinking the
whole a practical jest, and the final outburst of that
deep maternal love which is a part of every true
woman's passion, is great in its truth and simplicity.
Steep and unadorned is Vyasa's style, but at times it
has far more power to move and to reach the heart
than mere elaborate and ambitious poetry.[1]

IV. NALOPAKHYANAM AND THE RAMAYANA

It has been suggested above that some passages in the
story of Nala offer a great similarity with episodes of the
Ramayana. We will mention two of them.

The first one is Damayanti's lament — the passage on
which we have just quoted Sri Aurobindo. We present
here its parallel in Valmiki's Ramayana: Rama's lament
after he has discovered Sita's disappearance. As the reader
can see, there is a striking similitude between the two
monologues including that touch of delusion in which

---

1. Sri Aurobindo, Centenary Edition, Vol III (Pondicherry: Sri
Aurobindo Ashram, 1972), p. 159-161.

the lover's mind is so overwhelmed by pain that it wants to believe that the absence of the beloved is part of a game.

किं धावसि प्रिये नूनं दृष्टासि कमलेक्षणे ।
वृक्षैराच्छाद्य चात्मानं किं मां न प्रतिभाषसे ।।
तिष्ठ तिष्ठ वरारोहे न तेऽस्ति करुणा मयि ।
नात्यर्थं हास्यशीलासि किमर्थं मामुपेक्षसे ।।
पीतकौशेयकेनासि सूचिता वरवर्णिनि ।
धावन्त्यपि मया दृष्टा तिष्ठ यद्यस्ति सौहृदम् ।।
नैव सा नूनमथवा हिंसिता चारुहासिनी ।
कृच्छ्रं प्राप्तं न मां नूनं यथोपेक्षितुमर्हति ।।
व्यक्तं सा भक्षिता बाला राक्षसैः पिशिताशनैः ।
विभज्याङ्गानि सर्वाणि मया विरहिता प्रिया ।।

"Why do you run my darling? I saw you, O lotus-eyed one! You hide yourself behind the trees, why do you not answer me? Stay, tarry a while, O Sita with excellent limbs! Is there no compassion in your heart for me? You are not excessively given to fun; why then do you disregard me? You stand disclosed by your yellow silk garment, O lady with an excellent complexion! You have been seen by me even while running. Halt if you have any affection for me. Or it was definitely not Sita of charming smiles, who has most probably been killed; surely she could not have ignored me, fallen in adversity. Bereft of me, my youthful darling has evidently been devoured by flesh-eating ogres, dividing all her limbs among themselves."[1]

Another episode in the Nalopakhyanam reminds us of the Ramayana. This is the moment when Damayanti searches for Nala in the forest and is so desperate and has such a burning desire to speak about him that she asks the lion and the mountain whether they have seen her husband. Here she speaks to the lion:

पतिमन्वेषतीमेकां कृपणां शोककर्शिताम् ।
आश्वासय मृगेन्द्रेह यदि दृष्टस्त्वया नलः ।। **64.34**

"I am alone in this jungle searching for my husband, miserable, sorrow-stricken, o Lord of the beasts, if thou hast seen Nala, comfort me."

This passage is to be compared with many verses in the Aranyakanda of the Ramayana when Rama begs the whole forest, the trees and the animals to tell him whether they have seen Sita. Let us quote the verse in which Rama asks the lion about his wife.

शार्दूल यदि सा दृष्टा प्रिया चन्द्रनिभानना ।
मैथिली मम विस्रब्धः कथयस्व न ते भयम् ।।

"O lion, if you have seen my beloved with a face

---

1. Aranyakanda, 60, 26-30 in Srimad Valmiki-Ramayana, Part II (Gorakhpur: Gita Press, 1992), p. 814.

luminous like the moon, the princess of Mithila, tell me freely, do not be afraid." [1]

The expression of anguish is very similar in the two quotes, the only difference being that Rama as a man and a warrior has to reassure the lion that he will not harm him (*na te bhayam*). In both quotes, the style is direct, unadorned, moving in its simplicity.

It would be tempting to compare these passages, in Valmiki and in Vyasa, with yet another great piece of poetry, the lament of the king Pururavas in Kalidasa's play Vikramorvashiyam. When the nymph Urvashi in a spasm of jealousy leaves her mortal lover, she enters on proscribed ground and is transformed into a jasmine creeper. The king is desperately searching for her, and he addresses the elephant:

मदकल युवतिशशिकला गजयूथप यूथिकाशबलकेशी ।
स्थिरयौवना स्थिता ते दूरालोके सुखालोका । ।

"Lord of elephants, charming with the pride of youth, have you beheld that beautiful one, blooming with eternal youth, like the crescent Moon among women, her hair decked with the Yuthika flowers?"[2]

From this short quote, the reader can measure the great

1. Aranyakanda, 60, 25, in Srimad Valmiki-Ramayana, Part II (Gorakhpur: Gita Press, 1992), p. 813.
2. Kalidasa, Vikramorvashiyam, IV, 24.

distance that separates Kalidasa's play from the two epics. This verse is bursting with colours, images, epithets, similes, alliterations. The aesthetic possibilities contained in a king addressing an elephant are exploited to the full. So much so that one verse is not sufficient for Kalidasa to exhaust all this wealth. The address of the king to the elephant extends to several verses. There are descriptions of the elephant, the way he eats, the way he roars as if he were answering Urvashi's questions. Then the king compares himself, lord of kings, with the elephant, lord of his herd; he compares his wealth with the frontal ichor oozing from the elephant's temple; Urvashi with the elephant's mate, etc. Of course, here we are far from the austere self-restraint of Vyasa. If Vyasa was "a granite mind", Kalidasa was the "supreme poet of the senses". It mirrors the evolution of Indian civilisation and in a way, applied to literature, this is a very practical illustration of the different periods of India's development.

V. Sister Nivedita

The tale of Nala and Damayanti as reproduced in this monograph was written by Sister Nivedita in her small book *Cradle Tales of Hinduism*. The reader may be interested in knowing more about its author, an extraordinary woman who devoted her life to Mother India.

Sister Nivedita's original name was Margaret Elizabeth Noble. She was born in 1867 in Ireland. Margaret's grand-father, John Noble, was one of the Irish fighters for freedom. Her father was a minister of the Church who spent most of his time serving poor people. He died at 34 leaving his wife alone with three children. Margaret completed her education at the age of seventeen. Then in 1884, she went to England and became a teacher, first in a school at Keswick, and then at Wrexham and at Chester. She was very interested in new methods of teaching like those of Pestalozzi and Froebel. In 1892, she was invited to open a school of her own in Wimbledon, a suburb of London. In this way Margaret spent ten years as a teacher, from 1884 to 1894. A vivid description of her at that time, as given by a friend of hers, shows her as a young woman of medium height with bright grey-blue eyes, light golden brown hair, a radiant complexion and a charming smile. She was proud, generous and ardent. She knew how to

Sister Nivedita

inspire her students with enthusiasm. Within a short time she came to be known among the leaders of the intellectual society of London as a forward-looking educationist.

At that time she happened to read the life of the Buddha. For three years Margaret studied his teachings with reverence. Yet her thirst for Light and Truth was not quenched. Then something happened that was to change her whole life. A "Hindu Yogi" had arrived in London. His name was Swami Vivekananda.

In 1893 Vivekananda had gone to America to attend the Parliament of Religions. When the Parliament was over, Vivekananda lectured and taught in many parts of America. In 1895 he arrived in London where he had been invited by some English friends. He gave many lectures there and in a few days became well known.

A friend of Margaret, Lady Isabel Margesson one day invited Swami Vivekananda to her house. Margaret was present and was very impressed by the talk. Vivekananda left England and went back to America. About one year later, he came back to England and stayed there for eight months, giving many talks and classes. Margaret did not miss any of his lectures. She was deeply touched and learnt a lot from him. Yet she could not accept all his views. She argued with him, and fought with him. But Vivekananda had plans for her. One day during the question-answer session, the Swami suddenly rose and thundered, "What the world wants today is twenty men and women who can dare to stand in the street yonder and say that they possess nothing but God. Who will go?"

Another day, he was talking about the women of India, and their lack of education. He turned to Margaret and said, "I have plans for the women of my own country in which you, I think, could be of great help to me."

These words had a strange effect on her. She felt that it was a call — the call for which she had been waiting for all these years. Her mind was made up. She would join Vivekananda's army.

The Swami let England in December 1896. He knew that in India Margaret would have to face many difficulties. The English would hate her for befriending Indians. And

the Indians would doubt her good intentions. He made
all this clear to her in a letter. But then he made her a
promise: "I will stand by you unto death... the tusks of the
elephant come out but never go back, so are the words of
a man who never retracted."

Margaret arrived in Calcutta in January 1898. For some
time she lived with two American ladies who were also
Vivekananda's disciples. They stayed at Belur, a few miles
from Calcutta, in a cottage belonging to the monks of the
Ramakrishna order. The Swami came to the cottage every
morning. He would speak to the three women about his
ideals and his work. He would talk to them about India
and her people. He told them stories about devotees and
saints, about heroes and kings, and about the purity and
sacrifices of noble women. Soon Margaret met Sri Sarada
Devi, Sri Ramakrishna's companion. Vivekananda gave
Margaret a new name: Nivedita, which means "one who is
dedicated or offered to God". In the summer of that year,
they all travelled to Almora in the Himalayas. On the way
the Swami would tell them of the hard life of the villagers
and of their kindness to monks. From Almora they went
to Kashmir, passing through the land of Punjab. Nivedita
undertook the pilgrimage to Amarnath alone with her
guru. This was a profound experience for her.

She would listen to Vivekananda, sometimes she would
argue with him, sometimes she had doubts and was in

deep anguish. Sometimes she wanted to break away from him. Slowly she learned to meditate; she learned to be humble.

In a house situated opposite of that of Sarada Devi, Nivedita opened a school for girls (November 1898). She started her work earnestly. She taught the little girls reading and writing and introduced painting, clay-work and sewing. The following March, bubonic plague raged in Calcutta. Swami Vivekananda immediately set his monks and followers to work. They formed a plague service and Nivedita was in charge of it. She worked tirelessly day and night. The District Medical Officer will later write in his report, "During this calamity the compassionate figure of Sister Nivedita was seen in every slum of the Baghbazar locality. She helped others with money without giving a thought to her own condition. At one time when her own diet consisted only of milk and fruits, she gave up milk to meet the medical expenses of a patient."

In 1899 Nivedita travelled to England and then to America in an effort to raise funds for her school. Her guru travelled with her. In America and in England, Nivedita gave many lectures on India and Indian women.

She came back to India, this time as if she were returning to her own motherland. Now she called India "our country" and Indians "our people". Rabindranath Tagore would remark later, "When she uttered the words *our people*, the tone of absolute kinship which struck the ear was not heard from any other among us."

She re-opened her school and could earn some desperately needed money by writing books and giving lectures.

In 1902 Vivekananda passed away.

The death of the Swami had strengthened Nivedita's resolve to throw herself heart and soul into her work for India. Up till that time she had spent all her energy on her school work. She now decided to lend support to other causes as well, for the national movement in favour of political independence was rapidly growing. For this purpose she resigned from the Ramakrishna mission and plunged into the nationalist struggle. If an unjust law was passed by an Indian Council or Assembly, she was the first to speak against it. She was not afraid of the British Government and spoke what was in her mind. Soon she came to be a great influence in Bengal. She was one of those patriots for whom the youth had great respect. She told them once, "The good of your country should be your true aim... Think that the whole country is your country and your country needs work. Struggle for knowledge, for strength, for happiness and prosperity. Let all these be your aim in life. By no means, be found sleeping when the cry comes for battle." She fought for the ideal of a national education based on Indian culture, Indian values, Indian spirit. One of her great interest was in the revival of ancient Indian art. Among her friends were the great artists of the Bengal renaissance, Abanindranath Tagore and Nandalal Bose. Another of her dreams was the blossoming of Indian science. She encouraged her friend, the great scientist Jagadish Chandra Bose, to publish his important book *Plant Response*.

Sister Nivedita believed that India was the land of great women and she believed that once the women of India awoke the country would rise again. In this context, it is not surprising that she wanted to tell the story of one of the most heroic and pure of Indian women, Damayanti.

Sri Aurobindo had first met Sister Nivedita in Baroda when she came to give some lectures there. Sri Aurobido was then the secretary of the Maharaja of Baroda. When Sri Aurobindo started his revolutionary work in Bengal, they collaborated, trying to unite all the existing underground groups under a single organisation. When in 1910 Sri Aurobindo left Calcutta guided by an inner voice, he asked Sister Nivedita to take up the editing of the English weekly, the Karmayogin, in his absence. She consented and from that time onward she had the whole conduct of the paper till its closure.

She had known for some time that she was not to remain very long on this earth. On October 13, 1911, she passed away in Darjeeling.

Among her books, the best known is *The Master as I saw Him*, a book on Swami Vivekananda. She wrote also *Kali the Mother, Shiva and Buddha, Cradle Tales of Hinduism and Myths of the Hindus* and *Buddhists*.

VI. THE NAISADHACHARITA AND THE KANGRA PAINTINGS

a) The Naishadhacharita

It is perhaps proper to add here a few words about one of the most famous poems on Nala's story after the Nalopakhyanam of Mahabharata, upon the early part of which it is clearly based: the great *kavya* of the 12th century, the Naishadhacharita by Sriharsa.

Sriharsa was a poet at the court of the King of Kanyakubja. Innumerable stories and legends testify to his great *panditya*, or scholarship. His father is said to have been defeated in a scholarly duel, *shastrartha*, by another poet, following which he charged his son with the task of avenging him. Sriharsa then went on acquiring knowledge ceaselessly and learning from every possible pandit till he felt confident to return to the court of his father's patron where he was recognized as the greatest of poets. Sriharsa is said to have produced a great many works but his most famous *kavya* is the Naishadhacharita. The story goes that the King wanted the poet to go to Kashmir to have his work approved by Sarasvati, the goddess of learning, who presided there in person. Sriharsa proceeded to Kashmir and there received Saraswati's blessings, but not before having a learned argument even with her.

Sriharsha's language is considered to be extremely sophisticated. The entire Naishadhacharita with its 22 cantos containing more than 20000 verses is an occasion for a dazzling exercise in the display of virtuosity. He employs *chandas* of the most complex variety. Of his encyclopaedic knowledge there is plenty of evidence throughout. One example will be sufficient for the reader to measure the dexterity of the writer: during Damayanti's Swayamvar, the goddess Sarasvati describes the four gods seated next to Nala. But since she does not wish to disclose their identity, she provides a description of each person in words which can have at least two meanings. When she describes Indra, for example, read in one way the verse is applicable to Indra, but read in another, it is equally descriptive of Nala.

However the most important point to note here is that the

Naishadhacharita carries the story only through the honey-moon at Nishadha. It starts and ends as a love story. Nala's loss of his throne, his vicissitudes and separation from Damayanti upto his final reunion with her and his reinstatement are absent. The fault of Nala, which gives the opportunity for Kali to enter him and wreck his life and happiness, never occurs. The poem has only kept the "fairy tale" aspect and the *sringar rasa* is the dominating flavour all throughout. The poet describes at great length the happiness of the young married couple and the text closes on a beautiful scene of Nala and Damayanti looking at the moon from the veranda of their palace.

The reason we have chosen to refer to this poem in particular is because it has inspired a series of miniatures said to be amongst the most refined and delicate of all Indian paintings.

Of course the illustration of the Nala and Damayanti story did not start with the poem of Sriharsa. A Gujarati manuscript of the 15th century was based on a poem called Nalacampu of Trivikrama Bhatta. A Mahabharata

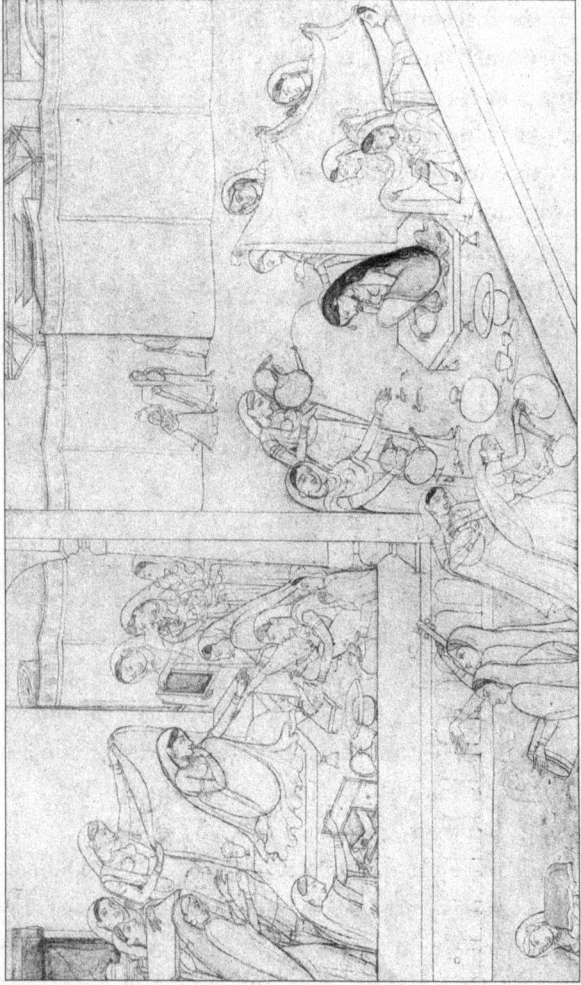

Damayanti's maidens adorning her (Museum of Fine Arts, Boston)

manuscript of the 16th century contains illustrations of the Nalopakhyanam. But by far, the most well-known series of paintings closely follows the Naishadhacharita text: this is a series of 48 drawings, 29 of which are in the Museum of Fine Arts, Boston, and form part of the great collection of Rajput pictures gathered by Dr. Ananda Coomaraswamy. A second series based upon the same text has surfaced later and is presently in the Jammu Museum.

b) The Coomaraswamy drawings

This series of drawings dates from the latter part of the 18th century and is attributed to painters of the Kangra state under the enlightened patronage of Raja Sansar Chand (1775-1823), a king who had many artists in his employ. Except for one or two, these pictures represent unfinished Kangra paintings similar to many others of their kind (perhaps master-sketches kept in the family of the Pahari artists and which served as models, *namoonas*, for subsequent pictures). The series in fact consists largely of drawings executed in bistre with a fine brush, and although colour is indicated in many of them they illustrate the art of pure drawing. Their style is known as "Kangra kalam"[1] (brush, style), and was at its height

---

1. According to Dr. Ananda Coomaraswamy, the famous art historian, Rajput painting in general is the painting of Rajputana and part of

during the reign of this King.

Here is how Dr. Coomarawamy, who in 1910 was the first to draw attention to these master-pieces, speaks of them: "Many things are noteworthy in these drawings. The human figure is drawn with astonishing facility in every possible seated or standing pose, indicating immense practice and well stored memory on the part of the artists. The figures are alert and eager; whole groups are animated by a single sentiment. ... The quality of the brush outline is most alluring. It is swift and effortless. In many places it attains a singular simplicity; there is a fondness of forms bounded by almost geometrical curves, which again pass into nearly straight lines... It is indeed remarkable how apparently a simple outline, carried round a whole figure, without raising the brush, avails to suggest the living form beneath the drapery." Coomarawamy was reminded of the Buddhist frescoes, "The outline is continuous and made with long strokes of the brush, as at Ajanta." He was fascinated in particular by the drawing of the feminine figures: "... The great work of the school was to create a feminine type peculiar to itself, and of infinite charm; not robust, like the Rajasthani types, but slender, and moving with an irresistible grace, intentionally accentuated by the long flowing lines of the drapery. Nothing, indeed, is more characteristic of the style than its use of flowing,

Central India and Pahari, that is, the regions of the Punjab Himalayas and Garhwal, including the Kangra valley. Since Dr. Coomaraswamy's work, much research has gone into identifying the diverse styles grouped under the general name of Rajput painting.

Boston drawings
Top: the honey-moon, Nala shows the night sky to Damayanti.
Bottom: Nala returns to Nishada after the marriage.

The gods go back to heaven after the swayamvara. Going the opposite way is Kali (chariot drawn by dogs)

unbroken lines, not ingeniously calligraphic like later Persian, nor boldly allusive like those of the early Rajasthani school, but creating a pure melody."[1] This supple grace of figures, Coomarswamy defines thus: "... every action is spontaneous and impulsive, and the whole energy of being enters into every movement. And thus

1. For Coomaraswamy, Rajput paintings (which he divided into two broad groups, the work produced in Rajasthan — Rajasthani, and the other produced in the Himalayan hill states — Pahari) was a separate development from the Mughal school and relatively free from its influences, emphasizing as it did the abstract and the ideal rather than the naturalistic and academic. In the course of his studies, he demonstrated the fact that all these paintings were a natural product of the so-called Western Indian style, which in turn was clearly derived from classical Indian painting of the fifth century, thus establishing the essential continuity of Indian painting.

Damayanti, painting by Bengali artist Nandalal Bose

the human figures of the Pahari painters are veritably god-like, in the sense of Bharata, who says that the actions of the gods spring from the natural disposition of the mind, while those of men depend upon the conscious working of the will."

The actions of the human figures *spring from the natural disposition of the mind*. What does it mean except that the body painted on the canvas is the direct representation of an inner state? Here we are touching upon the unique character of Indian painting and the peculiar appeal of this art, which springs from the remarkably inward, spiritual and psychic turn which was given to it by the pervading genius of Indian culture. As Sri Aurobindo says,

> In the treatment of the human figure all corporeal filling in of the outline by insistence on the flesh, the muscle, the anatomical detail is minimised or disregarded: the strong subtle lines and pure shapes which make the humanity of the human form are alone brought into relief; the whole essential human being is there, the divinity that has taken this garb of the spirit to the eye, but not the superfluous physicality which he carries with him as his burden. It is the ideal psychical figure and body of man and woman that is before us in its charm and beauty. The filling in of the line is done in another way; it is effected by a disposition of pure masses, a design

and coloured wave-flow of the body, bhanga, a
simplicity of content that enables the artist to flood
the whole with the significance of the one spiritual
emotion, feeling, suggestion which he intends to
convey, his intuition of the moment of the soul, its
living self-experience.

The "wave-flow" of the body is best illustrated in the drawings mentioned above, as the reader can see in the few illustrations presented here.

c) The Jammu Museum paintings

The most important of the painted material, and which has come to light relatively recently (in the mid-fifties) is a set of forty-seven paintings in the Karan Singh collection and exhibited at the Amar Mahal Museum of Jammu. Dr. Karan Singh recalls how an old painter Pandit Kunjlal Vaid, living in Basohli, gave him the priceless series: "Although his health was advanced — he [Pandit Kunjlal Vaid] must have been over 80 at the time — his eyes were keen and his speech clear. He met me with great affection and, to my surprise, placed before me a parcel wrapped in a large square handkerchief. He undid the cloth and, one by one, showed me the exquisite paintings with loving care. He said that many foreigners had come to him wanting to buy the collection but he had not agreed to part with it. Now that he was old and had no children, he would like to present the paintings to me." Dr Karan Singh accepted the gift which is now displayed in the first hall of the museum in Jammu.

The achievement of the artist who created these marvels is beautifully described by Dr B.N. Goswamy's opening words in his book *Pahari Paintings of the Nala-Damayanti Theme*:

> *Somewhere, among the many concerns of the Indian artist, there is also a concern with reaching the ultimate in the expression of delicacy of feeling. There are periods in which there is even a conscious search for the extreme: the idea becomes something of a gentle passion. One sees it in that inaudibly soft but clearly articulated note of music that trembles in the air for but a brief moment before it gets merged in the body of a raga. One sees it as Krishna massages the feet of Radha with the tenderest rose flower and as Radha puts out her hand to stop him, for its touch she says is too coarse for the soles of her feet. One sees it again in the poet bending down to hear the cataka, that delicate whisper of sound that the bud makes as it spreads out its petals in the fugitive moment of blossoming. One sees it also in the wispy softness of line in paintings like those in this book in which the brush seems barely to touch the surface, and forms*

look as if they have been 'breathed' upon paper.

Human forms that have been "breathed" on paper: what a striking expression to describe the art of the Indian painter. As Sri Aurobindo says, "In reality the shapes he paints are the form of things as he has seen them in the psychical plane of experience: these are the soul-figures of which physical things are a gross representation and their purity and subtlety reveals at once what the physical masks by the thickness of its caring."

VII. E. Arnold's Translation

Edwin Arnold (1832-1904) was among the most highly-regarded English poets of his day. After serving as principal of the government Sanskrit College in Pune, India, he joined the staff of the London Daily Telegraph as a journalist. He is best known for his book *The Light of Asia*, a blank verse epic about the life and teaching of Buddha. In his later years, he lived in Japan.

Edwin Arnold had great admiration for the epics of India. He writes, "There exist two colossal, unparalleled, epic poems in the sacred language of India, the Mahabharata and the Ramayana... These remarkable poems contain almost all the history of ancient India, so far as it can be recovered, together with such inexhaustible details of its political, social and religious life, that the antique Hindu world really stands epitomized in them."

Arnold translated portions of the Mahabharata, and in particular the story of Nala and Damayanti, attempting, as he says "to reproduce the swift march of narrative and old-world charm of the Indian tale". The reader will judge. We reproduce here a passage from Arnold's translation. This extract recounts the return of Nala to the kingdom of Vidarbha.

The news of Damayanti's second Swayamvara has just reached Ayodhya, where Nala lives under the name of Vahuka and serves the king Rituparna as a charioteer. This extract ends with a beautiful description of the horses, peacocks and elephants trumpeting their joy as they sense Nala's return and the imminence of Victory.

The evil being Kali, spying on Nala and waiting for an opportunity to take possession of him

Now when the Raja Rituparna heard
Sudêva's words, quoth he to Vâhuka
Full pleasantly: "Much mind I have to go
Where Damayanti holds Swayamvara,
If to Vidarbha, in a single day,
Thou deemest we might drive, my charioteer!"

Of Nala, by his Raja thus addressed,
Torn was the heart with anguish; for he thought:
"Can Damayanti purpose this? Could grief
So change her? Is it not some fine device
For my sake schemed? Or doth my Princess seek,
All holy as she was, this guilty joy,
Being so wronged of me, her rash weak lord?
Frail is a woman's heart, and my fault great!
Thus might she do it, being far from home,
Bereft of friends, desolate with long woes
Of love for me, — my slender-waisted one
Yet no, no, no! she would not, — she that is
My children's mother! Be it false or true,
Best shall I know in going; therefore now
The will of Rituparna must I serve."

Thus pondering in his mind, the troubled Prince
With joined palms meekly to his master said,
"I shall thy hest accomplish! I can drive

In one day, Raja, to Vidarbha's gates."
Then in the royal stables — steed by steed,
Stallions and mares, Vâhuka scanned them all,
By Rituparna prayed quickly to choose.
Slowly he picked four coursers, under-fleshed,
But big of bone and sinew; fetlocked well
For journeying; high-bred, heavy-framed; of blood
To match the best, yet gentle; blemish-free;
Broad in the jaw, with scarlet nostrils spread;
Bearing the Avarthas[1], the ten true marks, —
Reared on the banks of Indus, swift as wind.
Which, when the Raja looked upon, he cried,
Half-wrathful: "What thing thinkest thou to do?
Wilt thou betray me?
How should sorry beasts,
Lean-ribbed and ragged, take us all that way,
The long road we must swiftly travel hence?"
Vâhuka answered: "See on all these four
The ten sure marks: one curl upon each crest,
Two on the cheeks, two upon either flank,
Two on the breast, and on each crupper one.
These to Vidarbha — doubt it not — will go
Yet, Raja, if thou wilt have others, speak;
And I shall yoke them."

---

1. These are spots where the hair curls round, as upon the crown of
the human head.

Rituparna said:
"I know thou hast deep skill in stable-craft;
Yoke therefore such four coursers as thou wilt,
But quickly!"
Thus those horses, two by two,
High-mettled, spare, and strong, Prince Nala put
Under the bars; and when the car was hitched,
And eagerly the Raja made to mount,
At sign the coursers bent their knees, and lay
Along the earth. Then Nala, (O my King!)
With kindly voice cheering the gaunt bright steeds,
Loosed them, and grasped the reins, and bade ascend
Varshneya: so he started, headlong, forth.

At cry of Vâhuka the four steeds sprung
Into the air, as they would fly with him;
And when the Raja felt them, fleet as wind,
Whirling along, mute sat he and amazed;
And much Varshneya mused to hear and see
The thundering of those wheels; the fiery four
So lightly held; Vâhuka's matchless art.
"Is Mâtali, who driveth Indra's car,
Our charioteer? for all the marks of him
Are here! or Sâlihotra can this be,
The god of horses, knowing all their ways,
Who here in mortal form his greatness hides?

Or is it — can it be — Nala the Prince,
Nala the steed-tamer?" Thus pondered he:
"Whatever Nala knew this one doth know.
Alike the mastery seems of both; alike
I judge their years. If this man be not he,
Two Nalas are there in the world for skill.
They say there wander mighty powers on earth
In strange disguises, who, divinely sprung,
Veil themselves from us under human mould;
Bewilderment it brings me, this his shape
Misshapen, — from conclusion that alone
Withholds me; yet I wist not what to think,
In age and manner like, — and so unlike
In form! Else Vâhuka I must have deemed
Nala, with Nala's gifts."

So in his heart
Varshneya, watching, wondered, — being himself
The second charioteer. But Rituparna
Sat joyous with the speed, delightedly
Marking the driving of the Prince: the eyes
Attent; the hand so firm upon the reins
The skill so quiet, wise, and masterful
Great joy the Maharaja had to see.
By stream and mountain, woodland-path and pool,
Swiftly, like birds that skim in air, they sped;

Till, as the chariot plunged, the Raja saw
His shoulder-mantle falling to the ground;
And — loath to lose the robe — albeit so pressed,
To Nala cried he, "Let me take it up;
Check the swift horses, wondrous charioteer;
And bid Varshneya light, and fetch my cloth."
But Nala answered: "Far it lies behind;
A yojana already we have passed;
We cannot turn again to pick it up."

A little onward Rituparna saw
Within the wood a tall Myrobolan
Heavy with fruit; hereat, eager he cried,
"Now, Vâhuka, my skill thou mayst behold
In the Arithmic. All arts no man knows;
Each hath his wisdom, but in one man's wit
Is perfect gift of one thing, and not more.
From yonder tree how many leaves and fruits,
Think'st thou, lie fall'n there upon the earth?
Just one above a thousand of the leaves,
And one above a hundred of the fruits;
And on those two limbs hang, of dancing leaves,
Five crores exact; and shouldst thou pluck yon bough,
Together with their shoots, on those twain boughs
Swing twice a thousand nuts and ninety-five!"

Vâhuka checked the chariot wonderingly,
And answered: "Imperceptible to me
Is what thou boastest, slayer of thy foes
But I to proof will put it, hewing down
The tree, and, having counted, I shall know.
Before thine eyes the branches twain I'll lop:
How prove thee, Maharaja, otherwise,
Whether this be or be not? I will count
One by one — fruits and leaves — before thee, King;
Varshneya, for a space, can rein the steeds."

To him replied the Raja: "Time is none
Now to delay."
Vâhuka answered quick
(His own set purpose serving): "Stay this space,
Or by thyself drive on! The road is good,
The son of Vrishni will be charioteer!"
On that the Raja answered soothingly:
"There is not in the earth another man
That hath thy skill; and by thy skill I look
To reach Vidarbha, O thou steed-tamer!
Thou art my trust; make thou not hindrance now
Yet would I suffer, too, what thou dost ask,
If thou couldst surely reach Vidarbha's gate
Before yon sun hath sunk."

Nala replied:
"When I have counted those vibhîtak boughs,
Vidarbha I will reach; now keep thy word."
Ill pleased, the Raja said: "Halt then, and count!
Take one bough from the branch which I shall show,
And tell its fruits, and satisfy thy soul."
So leaping from the car — eager he shore
The boughs, and counted; and all wonder-struck
To Rituparna spake: "Lo, as thou saidst
So many fruits there be upon this bough!
Exceeding marvellous is this thy gift,
I burn to know such learning, how it comes."

Answered the Raja, for his journey fain:
"My mind is quick with numbers, skilled to count;
I have the science."
"Give it me, dear Lord!"
Vâhuka cried: "Teach me, I pray, this lore,
And take from me my skill in horse-taming."
Quoth Rituparn — impatient to proceed
Yet of such skill desirous: "Be it so!
As thou hast prayed, receive my secret art,
Exchanging with me here thy mastery
Of horses."
Thereupon did he impart
His rules of numbers, taking Nala's too.

But wonderful! So soon as Nala knew
That hidden gift, the accursed Kali leapt
Forth from his breast, the evil spirit's mouth
Spewing the poison of Karkôtaka
Even as he issued. From the afflicted Prince
That bitter plague of Kali passed away;
And for a space Prince Nala lost himself,
Rent by the agony. But when he saw
The evil one take visible shape again, —
Free from the serpent's poison, — Nishadh's Lord
Had thought to curse him then; but Kali stood
With clasped palms, trembling, and besought the
  Prince.
Saying: "Thy wrath restrain, Sovereign of men
I will repay thee well. Thy virtuous wife,
Indrasen's angered mother, laid her ban
Upon me when thou didst forsake her; since
Within thee have I dwelled in anguish sore,
Tortured and tossed and burning, night and day,
With venom from the great snake's fang, which passed
Into me by thy blood. Be pitiful!
I take my refuge in thy mercy! Hear
My promise, Prince! Wherever men henceforth
Shall name thee before people, praising thee,
This shall protect them from the dread of me;
NALA shall guard from KALI, if so now

Thou spare to curse me, seeking grace of thee."
Thus supplicated, Nala stayed his wrath,
Acceding; and the direful Kali fled
Into the Wounded tree, possessing it.
But of no eyes, save Nala's, was he seen,
Nor heard of any other; and the Prince,
His sorrows shaking off, when Kali passed,
After that numbering of the leaves, in joy
Unspeakable, and glowing with new hope,
Mounted the car again, and urged his steeds.
But from that hour the tall Myrobolan,
Possessed by Kali, stood there, sear and dead.

Then onward, onward, speeding like the birds,
Those coursers flew; and fast and faster still
The glad Prince cheered them forward, all elate:
And proudly rode the Raja toward the walls
Of high Vidarbha. Thus did journey down
Exultant Nala, free of trouble now,
Quit of the evil spell, but bearing still
His form misshapen, and the shrunken limb.

At sunset in Vidarbha (O great King!)
The watchers on the walls proclaimed, "There comes
The Raja Rituparna!" Bhima bade
Open the gates; and thus they entered in,

Making all quarters of the city shake
With rattling of the chariot-wheels. But when
The horses of Prince Nala heard that sound,
For joy they neighed, as when of old their lord
Drew nigh. And Damayanti, in her bower,
Far off that rattling of the chariot heard,
As when at time of rains is heard the voice
Of clouds low thundering; and her bosom thrilled
At echo of that ringing sound. It came
Loud and more loud, like Nala's, when of old,
Gripping the reins, he cheered his mares along.
It seemed like Nala to the Princess then, —
That clatter of the trampling of the hoofs;
It seemed like Nala to the stabled steeds
Upon the palace-roof the peacocks heard
And screamed; the elephants within their stalls
Heard it and trumpeted; the coursers, tied,
Snorted for joy to hear that leaping car;
Peacocks and elephants and cattle stalled
All called and clamored with uplifted heads,
As wild things do at noise of coming rain....

VIII. BIBLIOGRAPHY

— Arnold, Edwin. *Indian Idylls of the Mahabharata*. Boston: 1907.

— Sri Aurobindo. *The Problem of the Mahabharata*, in Centenary Edition, Vol. III. Pondicherry: Sri Aurobindo Ashram, 1972.

— Sri Aurobindo. *The Foundations of Indian Cult ure*, Centenary Edition, Vol. XIV. Pondicherry: Sri Aurobindo Ashram, 1972.

— Goswamy, B.N. *Pahari Paintings of the Nala-Damayanti theme*. New Delhi: Publications Division, Ministry of Information and Broadcasting, GoI, 1995.

— Eastman, A.C. *The Nala-Damayanti Drawings*. Boston: Museum of Fine Arts, 1959.

— Goswamy, B.N & Fischer, Eberhard. *Pahari Masters*. Zurich: Artibus Asiae Publishers, 1992.

— Mahabharata, original Sanskrit with Hindi translation (6 volumes), (the reader will find the Nalopakhyanam in the second volume, pp 1091 to 1164). Gorakhpur: Gita Press.

— Mackenzie, Donald A. *Indian Myth and Legend*. New Delhi: Smriti Books, 2000.

— Sister Nivedita, *Cradle Tales of Hinduism*. Calcutta: Advaita Ashrama, 1998.

The Gods talk to Nala into being their emissary to Damayanti, to plead their cases with her. Indra is their spokesman and Nala is shown with folded hands. Varuna, Yama and Agni stand behind Indra.